Women Speak
Life for Clonakilty women in the 1900's

Volume 1

Stories gathered by

Alison Wickham to celebrate

400 years of Clonakilty's history as a town.

© Alison Wickham June 2013

Cover Information

Handwriting by Margaret Feen: a page from her story, written in the 1980's.

Photograph of Mary O'Donovan (Taylor) O'Regan: was kindly loaned by the O'Regan family. It was taken in 1928 in Boston, when Mary was 18 years old. Mary endured a long sea journey to join her sister in Boston, but after less than 12 months was recalled home to mind her sick mother. She lived at 36 McCurtain Hill, Clonakilty and with her husband Ted O'Regan raised three children, James (Jimmy), Aiden and Joan. She passed away in 2005 in her mid nineties.

Published by
  Wickham Books
  3 Old Chapel Lane
  Clonakilty, County Cork
  Ireland
Email **abwickham@gmail.com**
Copyright © **Alison Wickham 2013**
ISBN **978-0-9926815-0-0**

Chapters

Forward 5
Frances Harrington 8
Mrs K 14
Jennifer Sleeman 17
Noreen Minihan 22
Mary Ruth McCarthy 27
Peggy 34
Hannah 37
Woodfield Days 39
Child of the 1940's 42
A West Cork Farmer's Wife 44
An Educator 48
A Former Pupil 51
Dena O'Donovan 54
Growing up in Rural West Cork in the Nineteen Twenties 58
   Forward by Margaret Feen *59*
   My Own Place *61*
   School Days *62*
   Photograph *64*
   Heart of the Home *65*
   Entertainment *67*
   Meitheal Memories *69*
   Summer jobs *74*
   Fish and Fowl *76*
   Fun and Games *78*
   The Village shop *79*

Travelling visitors 81
St James Day 82
The Feast of Feasts 83
Friends and neighbours 86
Memories, Memories 88
1934 89
Lightning Strike 92

Rites of Passage 95
Birth 95
Marriage 97
Death 98

Legislation Affecting Women and Children in the Twentieth Century 100

The Role of the ICA in Improving the Lives of Irish Women 101

Women, tea and soda bread 102

Miscellaneous Quotes 104

Forward

I am a Blow-In[1] to Clonakilty, County Cork, Ireland, brought here from my homeland, New Zealand, by my husband's career. We arrived early in 1998 when Ireland was three years into the Celtic Tiger Economy, a period of rapid economic growth after years of hardship.

Clonakilty was still very much a small town serving the local agricultural community. It was primarily mono-cultural with traffic in both directions on the narrow main street, limited shopping, and very few houses for sale. I remember that cars were fewer and mostly very small, bicycles were still seen as goods delivery vehicles, and many people crossed themselves as they walked or cycled past the imposing Catholic Church.

All this has rapidly changed. Over the past fifteen years I have watched Clonakilty blossom into a thriving modern town with excellent amenities and a population doubled to over four thousand. All achieved without losing its innate charm and community spirit. Its forward thinking, civic pride and resilience have made it an attractive place to live for locals and many others from around the world who now call it home. The striking beauty of the local rural and coastal scenery also deserve mention.

Lately I have become aware of how little has been documented of the lives of Irish women and girls compared to those of men, and compared to women in the other places that I have lived: New Zealand and America. Given that 2013 is the 400th anniversary of Clonakilty town, I was motivated to collect personal anecdotes that illustrated the experiences of women who lived in the area in the twentieth century, before their

---

[1] West Cork term for a newcomer.

stories were lost. Their lives were so different to those of today with much more hard physical work involved in raising a large family and ensuring their needs were met, as well as supporting the man of the house. I also wanted to acknowledge the contributions to society at large that they made in the course of doing so.

This collection of stories is, with a few exceptions, from women aged in their 60's to mid 90's. All these tales, unless otherwise noted, were told to me first-hand by women living within fifteen kilometres of Clonakilty. I preferred to gather a diversity of experiences that would illustrate aspects of women's lives of the times, rather than full histories, and the stories often shed light on the women of previous generations also. In most cases we talked and I took notes, which I typed and the women edited for accuracy. If anyone chose to use a pen name, that was perfectly acceptable. I have illustrated it with photos I have taken locally recently, some of museum items and a few family photos that I have scanned. Due to past hard times most women did not have artefacts relating to their personal history that I could access.

I see this small collection as just a beginning, and I hope that it will inspire other women to come forward and share more reminiscences and insights into the ordinary, yet extraordinary, lives they have led.

This self-generated and self-published project has been a personally fulfilling experience for me as I have come to a deeper understanding that the differences between the lives of women in Ireland, and of those in my homeland and different regions of the USA are almost entirely the result of the differences in the histories of the places. Histories created in the main by men, but lived through and forward into future generations by the women who raised them, bore their children and provided for their physical needs through the ages. For this, women deserve to be honoured through the recording of their lives.

I thank all my remarkable sources for their great generosity in sharing their lives with me and in particular to the superb written contribution of Margaret Feen, entitled *Journey into Another Life: Growing up in West Cork in the 1920's.* Thanks also to those who supported me in my project with encouragement, Irish translations and proof reading, and to my husband Brian.

Any profits from the sale of this volume, after costs have been met, will be donated to the Clonakilty Museum to further preserve and honour the lives of local women.

Alison Wickham, June 2013

Inchydoney Beach 2013

Frances Harrington

Uneventful, would be a word I would use to describe my life and the happiest days were those spent with my birth family and then my own family. I was born in 1921 in my parent's home in Clonakilty with the local doctor in attendance. He lived just two doors away. There was only one doctor in the town at that time: a very approachable, hard-working man out night and day, who sadly lived a short life:

We lived in a large, comfortable house on the main street. This was unusual in two respects; an extension to the house was a grocery store and a coal yard managed by an uncle, so our home had no garden at all: the yard was used for the horses and carts of customers. Secondly, my father was a farmer. My mother frequently said, 'I brought up seven children on the side of the street in Clonakilty, but we had acres just a mile down the road.'

My birth family included an older brother, two younger brothers, and two younger twin sisters. The youngest boy died at eighteen months of meningitis, which was prevalent at that time. I did not need to be a help to my mother as we had a country girl, who lived in. She started each day at 6am and kept the coal range going and cooked the meals for the family. She also did the majority of the laundry, most of which was done by hand in a large wooden tub. Items like towels were boiled and the special occasion tablecloths sent to the local laundry. Laundry was dried on lines in the yard out back. A second girl was employed to look after the twins. They were wheeled about in a double pram, not easy to manage on Clonakilty's narrow footpaths, which I discovered for myself when taking them for a walk.

I began my schooling at the age of five at the local convent. A very wrinkled old nun greeted us when we arrived, and so frightened me that I caused quite a stir. However, I settled into school life and remember enjoying drawing, playing with Plasticine[2] and energetic games of tig tag. Being the niece of the Monsignor was not always easy, and I vividly remember the humiliation I suffered when I was made an example of by a vindictive nun in front of my uncle, for missing my catechism. A sharp caning across the hands was also something that occurred rather more frequently than I would have liked.

My mother did not approve of us playing in the street or crossroads dancing, but we did have a simple little two-room place at Inchydoney [3] where we could stay. It was hard to sleep, as it was often too noisy from the wind. Sometimes we travelled there by pony and trap just to take tea and swim in our modest bathing costumes. There was little there then, apart from a big country house hotel.

In those days, confirmations only happened once every three or four years when the Bishop and his man came down from Cork. In my family we received bicycles for our confirmation, which gave us great mobility. My mother came from Bandon and we went there frequently for holidays by pony and trap, as there was no convenient route between Clonakilty and her family home by train.

As there was no girl's secondary school in Clonakilty, I went to live with my mother's sister in Cork and attended the Ursuline Convent Secondary School on Patricks Hill.

---

[2] A flexible modeling material invented in 1897.
[3] Inchydoney is a white sand beach on an island connected to the mainland by a causeway, built in The Famine times.

They were happy times there in a family with girls my age. I enjoyed playing hockey. It was not available in Clonakilty because there was a prejudice against English games and camogie[4], the GAA[5] girls' game, was rather rough. At 17 and a half years old I left secondary education, having not been pressed to do the matriculation exam. My mother thought it a good idea that I should go to cookery school at the Edinburgh College of Domestic Science, studying household management and high-class cookery. Another girl, who was a distant relative from Crookstown, travelled there with me. Together we boarded in the School for Catering. After I had completed the course my brothers said, 'What are you doing over there now there is a war[6] on?' They encouraged me to return home.

At Easter in 1942 I married at the age of 21, an uncommonly young age for a girl then. My husband was a Skibbereen man in his early thirties who practised law and we met in Clonakilty, where he had an office in town. (Pubs were not places for women to meet people then. The only time it was decent was after funerals, when a discreet glass of sherry might be sipped in the seclusion of the 'snug' or private bar.)

We travelled up to Cork to choose the engagement ring together and had the distinction of the first white wedding[7] in the Clonakilty church. My uncle, the Monsignor officiated with my two sisters as brides-maids. The hotel at Inchydoney Island was the setting for our wedding breakfast, which we reached by car. Wartime

---

[4] An Irish stick and ball team sport for girls, almost identical to hurling.
[5] Gaelic Athletic Association, founded in 1884 to foster Irish sports and nationalism.
[6] World War 2 : 1939-1946
[7] A wedding where the bride is dressed all in white.

ruled out a honeymoon in mainland Europe so we went to Dublin.

My husband was a good man who recognised how the legal system and the church kept women in Ireland down. He insisted that both our names should be on our legal ownership papers, not just the man's name as was customary. Women did not have chequebooks and most were reliant on housekeeping money doled out by their husband.

After our marriage we lived in the town at Astna Square (pictured in recent years above) in a house with a rented shop below and accommodation over. There was no backyard or land with it, so as our family grew to three children we moved out on to the Island Road. We had a big house with views of the bay, a vegetable garden and our own Jersey cow. I had household help but made butter for our own use and sold surplus to the local shops. We grew the things we could not buy from the store e.g., peas, French beans, leeks, as well as having chickens. The house had tap water indoors but it had to be hand pumped from our own well, as there was no electrification until the 1950's. Meals were cooked on the range but as coal was rationed, turf (often still wet) and timber, cut by my husband, were the main fuels available.

For entertainment lady friends would gather in ones or two's at 'At Homes'. We made sponge cakes from our own eggs and bought special white flour for them. Apple tart or apple cakes were also popular. Occasionally travelling players came to Clonakilty and there was also an active cinema. About once a week I walked from Youghals to Kilgarriffe to see my relations.

During World War 2 there were shortages of food like raisins, bananas and oranges along with white flour. My uncle's shop had to declare what foods were rationed, these included tea and sugar and even baby had a share. Irel coffee essence became the popular substitute for coffee. During this period we bought our clothing in Cork but my mother also made clothes on a hand operated sewing machine. When electrification finally arrived it was wonderful to no longer need the fragile and expensive Tilley lamps, which needed such care to move from room to room.

Our daughters went away to board at secondary school in Cork and our son to Holy Ghost in Dublin. After my eldest brother died my father and mother moved out to a house on The Miles. My mother, who lived to be 104, frequently cycled from there to see me at Youghals. Later she had an old Ford car, which she drove without making much use of the gears. As the car rattled complaining down our drive, my son used to amuse us by saying, 'Here comes the agony.'

Houses built by the local authority in mid century.

Mrs K

Life in Clonakilty began for me in 1947 and I married one year later at 20 years old. My husband, a carpenter, and I lived in a lodge on the Island Road at first. In the early 1950's we moved into a two bedroom semi-detached house in a new social housing estate. Our house was a very simple one when we moved in, just two rooms up and two down. There was an iron cooker fired by coal and wood in the main downstairs room (which we strung lines in front of for drying clothes in wet weather) and a little pantry with a sink off the other room. Upstairs there were two rooms with the only bathroom facility being a toilet bowl. Soon after moving in we installed an electric cooker and a bath. Over the years we added more rooms on to increase the convenience and comfort of the house. Nine children were born to us there.

Life was very hard by today's standards but I believe we were happier then. The community was a close one and very safe and supportive. Crime did not seem to be a problem to worry about. People did their best with what they had to hand and saved for the things they needed. Religion and church attendance were an important part of life, giving much comfort and guidance.

Except for the cooker household appliances did not exist. Our hands did all the work of meal preparation and mending and I did the laundry in the sink. After my husband met with an accident that disabled him, I had to support the family by working as a nurse's helper at the Mt Carmel hospital. Many were the times that I was hanging the washing out to dry at two in the morning, after the end of my shift. I loved my work with the patients at the hospital, especially nursing the men. I also looked after the nuns at night by helping them. They were always trying to get me to take over the meals for the hospital as they knew I could cook, but I was reluctant to leave the care of patients, because I loved it so much. However, one day a nun told me that God was calling me to do the cooking, and so I did.

I cooked for 50 or so patients with the help of another girl. We used a coal range to cook the food and sometimes it was necessary for us to get the coal ourselves if we didn't want the cooker to go out. Usually I arrived at work at about 7.30 am and together we prepared and cooked the breakfast of porridge, bread and tea. We then began preparations for the main meal of the day, dinner. This consisted of things like lovely ham or bacon with fresh vegetables. The floury potatoes were boiled in their skins and peeled by the patients themselves.

The nun who looked after the office served up the meals and the ward's maids carried these via the stairs to the patients, as there were no lifts in the hospital. The ward staff and nuns fed the less able patients first, at 12.30pm, and the rest of the patients had dinner at 1pm. In the afternoon my assistant and I could go back home for an hour or two. At 5.30pm a lighter tea was served, maybe a fry or a boiled egg, with bread and butter. Morning and afternoon tea consisted of tea or milk, with bread, biscuit or cake in the afternoon. We did all the cleaning up and washing of dishes by hand ourselves as there were no dishwashers. I usually got home by 6pm but sometimes it was later. I retired from this job at the age of 62 but continued to look after the elderly nuns several nights each week. In total it was for about 20 years. I would start work there at about 9pm and finish at 6.30am, catching up on my sleep during the day.

My older boys were a wonderful help to me when they were young. They took jobs in the town on holidays and weekends and contributed to the household budget. As they grew old enough my daughters were given jobs in the hospital in the school holidays. The nuns were very good to us.

All my children are alive and well in Ireland. Five of them are nurses.

Clonakilty Catholic church viewed from Bridge Street.

Jennifer Sleeman

Although I did not come to Ireland until the 1950's when my husband retired from the British Army, I have become the matriarch of a very Irish family. Five of my six children and their families live here and all six identify themselves as Irish.

At the time of my arrival here I was the young mother of three of my six children, after a childhood in South Africa and an early adulthood as an Army wife on the continent. We came to Ireland because it was the home of a very close friend of my husband's (they had been prisoners' of war together) and he recommended it as a good place to live. Certainly I would endorse this and have never for a moment been anything but grateful for the life we have here. My children are all staunchly Irish and love being so, as the Irish are always greeted as friends anywhere in the world.

Of course, initially, there were differences for me to get used to. When I had my fourth child in a nursing home in the late 1950's I was astonished that no one was breast feeding and that all the patients gathered to say the rosary together every night. In those days new mothers were not allowed to take baths and it was assumed that sleeping pills would be taken at night. My fifth child's normal birth was another surprise when I was anaesthetised for the birth without being consulted. However, we did feel very welcomed in Ireland and people were kind to us. I joined the ICA to get to know others and found the monthly meetings very friendly and informative.

When I was small we would say our simple prayers at night, but only when we visited my mother's people in Scotland did we go to church. I clearly remember the minister giving a very loud sermon, shouting, and thinking it must be me he was shouting at. I was terrified although I don't think I told anyone. God was someone we did not worry about until World War 2 came and my mother, with three children, sailed from South Africa to UK to join our father who was recalled to the Navy. We thought it would be a great adventure to be torpedoed and prayed each night that God would make this happen! How wise our mother was not to tell us what the reality of being torpedoed would be like and how good that our prayers were not answered.

During the war we went to the Church of England and when we moved north, to the Church of Scotland. I remember the first Sunday when there were no bells, as bells were to tell us the invasion had begun.

Back in South Africa post-war I now considered myself grown-up and I seemed to have been quite religious driving 14 miles to the little thatched Anglican Church on Sundays. The only thing I remember about that was an old lady sitting in front of me and the feather in her hat bobbing to the beat of her heart, and some pleasure in the prayers.

Then I married a Catholic and had to promise that the children would be brought up in the faith. I did notice the comfort and pleasure that my husband got from his religion and considered changing, but it was only when I came to live in North Cork that I found a priest who was interested enough to give me instruction. After a year of instruction and discussion with Father O'Neill every Tuesday evening I was received into the church. He was a wonderful old man; I loved him dearly and cried bitter tears at his funeral. I must state quite clearly that, as I am now and the church was then, I would not have joined, but I must have been different then.

In 1972 we moved to a house with a field in Ardfield. By then my sons were away at college, my older daughters boarding at school in Dunmanway and my youngest in the National School at Rathbarry. Over the years I kept hens, ducks, turkeys, goats, ponies and geese and found the hayshed useful for drying washing. It was important to me all my life to be self-sufficient, the way our family had been on the farm in South Africa. Even as a child I had kept my own rabbits and hens. So many people there would say, 'We got everything off the place' and it was something I aspired to which was not possible in the mobile Army life. I read John Seymour's book *Self Sufficiency* while at Ardfield and it made a big impression on me, and added to my intense interest in sustainability and taking care of the environment. Thinking back to the days of being a mother my life seemed to be full of growing food and preparing it for consumption by my family.

In Ardfield we took part in the 'Stations', the custom of hosting Mass in rotation around the farmhouses of the townland. How often the stations were held in your own home depended on how many Catholic families were in the farmhouses of the townland, but it was not expected of the cottages. It was about every ten years in our area at the time. At the last stations I held, the priest arrived when I had the pre-dinner nibbles arranged on the table and before the main course was out of the oven. 'Is this all we are going to eat?' he asked with concern. Stations were a great way of socialising with all your neighbours and everyone was invited to call in over the course of the day. The festivities would go on long after the Mass was said and the meal eaten. Far into the night visitors would be welcomed with food and drink.

I think to begin with I had Faith and the Church gave me sustenance, but slowly things began to change. I applied to CMAC (now known as ACCORD). This is where, very late in life, I gained confidence to be myself and that I had certain abilities, and for this opportunity I will always be grateful to the church.

Sadly as time went on into the 1980's, my husband's mind began to fail noticeably. Increasing forgetfulness and perhaps some depression resulted in being referred to a geriatrician. The diagnosis was delivered like a bombshell: it was Alzheimer's. And with nothing else said, we were shown the door. What to do? I was shell-shocked but wrote to my sisters in the UK and they sent me information. Later, I corresponded with the specialist we saw and explained how difficult it was to deal with such news without any information or support on the future, and coping offered. He agreed and apologised and thankfully things changed for the better. In those times it was hard to break the news to people about mental conditions. I remember one very nice man asking, 'How is the Colonel?' When I explained that something had gone very wrong with his mind he kindly said, 'What a sad thing to happen to such a nice gentleman.'

Meanwhile faith continued to fade and although I still go to Mass I wonder if I should. It all seems irrelevant in the overpopulated world (and here the church must bear some guilt) poised on environmental collapse. I find the Church is full of rules made up by old celibate men and has little to say to the present world and its problems.

There have been glimpses of what could be, Mass in Peru where I wept at the power of devotion tangible in the church. Mass in Knocknaheeny where my great friend Pat Fogarty is PP and where the Church feels welcoming and alive. Mass in Glenstal: the richness of the liturgy.

After my husband died I moved into Clonakilty town because I was on my own. It was one of the best things I ever did because for the first time in my adult life I came to feel that I belonged and was part of a real and vibrant community. I became involved in working to raise awareness in issues important to me and that has been a great source of satisfaction and new friendships.

Clonakilty Technical School

Noreen Minihan

My father was one of the first Garda Siochana in Clonakilty when he came to the barracks on Pearse St in 1922. It was on the site occupied today by Galwey's Pharmacy. My mother lived at 58 Pearse St and so they met and married and I was their firstborn child. Sadly, he died just four months later from pneumonia, brought on by getting thoroughly soaked while helping out at a time of flooding.

My mother ran a highly successful grocery business. Her entrepreneurial spirit expressed itself when she opened a restaurant in our dining room, behind the shop. It was a very busy venture, especially on Friday Market days and Fair days (which were held on the first Monday of the month) and required staff to help her. She was especially known for her cream cakes and tarts, bought from local bakeries. My grandmother, who lived with us, was a noted dressmaker and instructed girls in the art of dressmaking. When I was about six years old Mammy remarried a wonderful man and had five more children. After her death her shop was named Betty Brosnan's after her.

All my schooling took place in Clonakilty. The nuns were very good to me at secondary school. Knowing that it was all hands on deck to help out in the shop after school, they encouraged me to bring two lunches to school each day. This way, plus a sustaining cup of tea, I could stay on at school to study until 6pm. After completing my Leaving Certificate (a requisite for a career in teaching, nursing or the Civil Service: the main avenues open to women) I began my training at Mary Immaculate Teachers' Training College in Limerick. My teachers from Sacred Heart were delighted, as it was an honour for the school to have a pupil accepted there.

I started in 1949 and in those days the student teachers, all girls, lived in. There were 100 students, 50 junior and 50 senior. It was a very regimented and rather spartan life, up at 6.30am and to bed at 9.00pm. Another avenue into teaching for those not accepted into training college, was through becoming a Junior Assistant Mistress (JAM). In the Leaving Cert. year girls could take optional Easter oral exams. If you passed the exams, which covered English, Irish, needlework and singing, you could obtain teaching work in a school if the average number of pupils was low (say 8-10 students). The pay was less than that of a trained teacher, but in fact if student numbers were low, even a trained teacher only received the JAM salary.

My career as a teacher began at Knockskeagh School, about 7 kilometres from Clonakilty. My mother bought me a beautiful state of the art bicycle. It had three speed gears, a dynamo lamp, a basket in the front, a carrier at the back and a bicycle stand! It was the envy of all the pupils. To this day past pupils talk about my 'Merc' of a bike!

In 1955 I transferred to St Joseph's Infant Boys' School in Clonakilty. The Infant School consisted of three classes: Junior Infants (four and five year olds) Senior Infants (six) and First Standard (seven year olds). It was located in lovely old cut stone buildings in O'Rahilly Street, opposite Scoil na mBuachaillí today. In 1955 my class consisted of 56 junior and senior infant boys, with desks and seating for just 38! I managed to accommodate them by rotation, having some seated on the floor for listening tasks, some at the desks for written work and the rest standing for blackboard work. Because all the pupils started on their fourth birthday, in a later year just before the summer break, I had 62 children in the class. However, sometime later the system changed to one where all the children started at the beginning of the school year after they had turned four.

In 1957 the Public Service Marriage Bar was lifted for teachers and so when I married in 1959 I was able to continue. My husband, Michael, was a travelling representative for Deasy's Brewery, which at that time was bottling Guinness and manufacturing Deasy Minerals in premises under the arch and at the back of O'Donovan's Hotel on Pearse St. It later moved to what is now known as Deasy's Car Park and then to Cork. We had six children, three boys and three girls between 1960 and 1972 and I worked up until the day each baby was born. We got precisely six weeks maternity leave before we had to return to work. They were very busy years, but we had a housekeeper to help. I did all the knitting of jumpers and cardigans for the family in any moment where I was sitting down and also a great deal of sewing for the girls and the occasional special outfit for the boys. The play-pen was a very handy thing to have: I got into it myself with a small table, seat and my sewing machine.

In 1963 the Infant School moved to the new school buildings across the road and I became the Principal of the Infant School in 1967, a position I held until 1995. When the job of Principal of the amalgamated Infant and Senior School came up in 1995 I was offered the role, but instead chose to continue teaching for my final year as a permanent employee, before retirement in 1996. I continued on as a substitute teacher in various schools in West Cork, often at very short notice, until Michael took ill in 2008. Thus, I can say that I have taught many a local man under the age of 62 at some stage. It was a job I loved, particularly preparing the 7 year olds for their first Holy Communion. I now have the title of Diocesan Visitor, which involves talking to the pupils about what they have learned in the Religion Programme.

Alongside my career I was also involved as secretary for the Irish National Teachers Organisation from the day I left training college and was not relieved until I had four children.

My husband and I believed it important to take part in the local community and action groups enabling progress and improvements that benefit everyone both practically and socially. We were very involved in the Festivals of West Cork in the 1960's and 1970's and I was the Hostess in the highly popular Midnight Cabarets. Some of the more important activities I was part of were:

- From 1964 fundraising for the Cork Polio Aftercare group which over time became COPE
- The Children of Mary Catholic Religious Association
- Community fundraising for the building of the Clonakilty Community Hall which opened in 1983 at a cost of £379,000
- Clonakilty Tidy Towns, a chapter of a national organisation to stimulate pride of place for residents, workers and visitors from the end of the 1970's. I am currently President of Clonakilty Tidy Towns.
- CLOAG, the Clonakilty Local Organisation Action Group which helped Travellers out of crowded barrel topped roadside caravans and tents and into local authority houses. A preschool was also set up to assist the children to make friends before they got to school. Later state funding helped with training and the establishment of the Traveller's Centre.

- Training of boys and girls to serve at Mass and religious ceremonies.
- Organising a lottery to enable on-going funding for the Clonakilty Community Hospital and the local Community Hall.

Each of these organisations, thanks to all the willing workers involved, has made a positive contribution to the town and its people over the years as well as being a source of friendship and pleasure.

Emmet Square, Clonakilty 2012

Mary Ruth McCarthy

My father Sam Glanville was a lighthouse keeper, as was his father before him and we lived a somewhat roaming life as we moved about the Irish Coast. He and my mother Jo were from the south of Ireland; Michael my brother (born 1930), Martha my sister (born 1933) and I (born 1932) were all born near Kilkeel, Co. Down. A lighthouse keeper had to have experience of life at sea, or a trade, in order to undertake the training for light keeping and my father had both.

In 1936 we lived in Inishowen, Co. Donegal, then moved to Cobh, Co. Cork in 1939 where my father 'kept the light' on Spitbank in the harbour. Furnished dwellings were provided on site, for keepers' families, the exception being Cobh. Here we lived in rented accommodation. This consisted of a large house divided in two. I called it 'half a house', because another family occupied the other half. There was a large garden behind the house, very sheltered, so apple trees and fruit bushes thrived, and there was plenty of ground space to grow potatoes, onions carrots etc. In 1942 we moved to Skerries, Co. Dublin. The lighthouse was on Rockabill, some way off the Dublin coast.

In December of the same year we made our next and final move to Galley Head Lighthouse situated on a headland eight or nine miles from Clonakilty town, West Cork. Back then this location was seen as somewhat isolated and consequently backward. My mother was very concerned about Michael's secondary schooling. It was accepted in those days that a girl's further education was of less importance.

Near the houses at Galley Head there was a huge rainwater tank and a cold water tank in the pantry that had a sink. My mother cooked on the coal range in the kitchen. We also had a Scandinavian primus stove for quick cooking. She made delicious beef stews, Irish stews, and frequently cooked fish, mackerel or the less favoured pollock. My father caught the fish from a rowing boat with a friend, or from the rocks with rod but no reel. Although we ate rashers as a treat for Sunday breakfast, we seldom ate pork in any form, as there were disease concerns about its consumption at the time.

The only form of transport we had was my father's bicycle, my mother never cycled. She was taken to town once or twice a month in the local farmer's horse and cart, or occasionally in a pony and trap. My father wore a uniform provided, but clothes for the rest of the family came from Cash's and O'Mahoneys, drapers on Rossa Street. We did not have modern conveniences so we washed ourselves in a galvanised bath in front of the fire.

The Galley Head had a telephone line, possibly because of its coastal monitoring role in wartime. Occasionally a local person came to use the telephone to ask for the doctor or vet to be called out. The Second World War was raging in Europe at the time, although Ireland was not involved its Government co-operated with the Allies. There was rationing of clothes, tea, cigarettes etc.

The nomadic life we lived we enjoyed very much. This meant we attended 4 very different primary schools. All Michael ever wanted to do was 'go to sea' and following 2 years attendance (by bicycle) at St. Mary's Secondary School in Clonakilty, this is what he did. Martha died before her 15th birthday, this was a very sad time for us.

Following my father's retirement we continued to live in West Cork. I spent some years in England, first as a teacher in Kidderminster and then nurse training in

Birmingham, later returning to Ireland where I worked as a nurse.

My husband Jerry and I married in 1961, raising our six daughters and two sons in rural West Cork. Our great treat in those days was to take a picnic and go by car to the seaside often visiting Galley Head Lighthouse.

German Crew Ashore from U Boat: *A true story written by Mary Ruth about her memories of a real event.*

My father opened the door of the bedroom where Martha and I slept and, as if it were an everyday occurrence, said: 'There are German soldiers in Joe's house, do you want to see them?' This statement was beyond our understanding. Why were they in Joe's house? Why were they in Ireland? Germany, we understood, was at war with other countries somewhere in the world but not in Ireland. Bewildered we got out of bed and went with Michael and my mother into Joe's kitchen. The following are my impressions of that night. I was 13, Michael 15 and Martha was 12.

On the cliff-top, not far from the white-washed walls which surround the lighthouse at Galley Head, West Cork, stands a roofless small hut. This is what remains of a concrete lookout post and is one of many which were constructed on the coastline around Ireland in the 1940s. Men who knew the cliffs, inlets and shores of each particular place underwent a period of training and performed their duties, two at a time, day and night, as Coast Watchers. The hut had a telephone.

The assistant keeper at Galley Head was Joe O' Byrne who lived beside us with his wife and baby daughter. A third building called 'The Spare House' was alongside Joe's. A telephone was located there as well.

On the night of March 13th 1945 all of us, except my father, went to bed. He said: 'I will stay here in the kitchen for a short while.' That puzzled me as he was not on duty. Joe had lit the lantern at sunset and he would keep watch until sunrise. The man on duty stayed in a room in the tower or in his kitchen where the range was always lighting.

Sometime after we went to sleep a loud explosion woke us and our bedroom was flooded with a pink light. My mother came to reassure us. There was a second loud bang and more pink light. We were alarmed for a while but quietness ensued and we went back to sleep. Our second disturbance was my father telling us about the soldiers. Of course we wanted to see them.

We rushed to Joe's kitchen where we saw my father and Joe with five or six young men in uniform. The strangers were talking cheerfully together and did not have guns. From his experiences during World War I[8] my father had a smattering of French and German which enabled rudimentary conversation to take place. Soon afterward a Coast Watcher came with more uniformed Germans, making a total of eleven. All were happy to see each other. Joe's baby was brought in to be admired by the soldiers. One was their captain, according to my mother, and had children in his home country. They had scuttled their submarine U260 and made their way to the cliffs in a rubber dinghy. The pink light we had earlier seen was from flares set off by them.

'Which cliff?' I asked, since I had explored many of them being an agile cliff climber. My father said he did not know but I suspect he did. How did they manage to get

---

[8] 1914-1918

safely up the cliffs? Their uniforms, as far as I could tell, were not wet with seawater.

We took a great interest in the discussion as to what food to give them. Tea was rationed and very precious. It was decided to give them coffee because they were 'from the continent' and were accustomed to that and not to tea. Ground coffee was not available. Irel coffee was made with boiling water added to the sweet syrupy essence. What food they were given I cannot remember. The 'Cork Examiner' with EIRE printed on it was shown to them and they were delighted. The men knew Ireland was neutral.

All the while my mother and the three of us were observing and enjoying the excitement. Either my father, or Joe or a Coast Watcher, telephoned the authorities somewhere to inform them of the situation. There were procedures to be followed in an event like this at the Galley; there had been similar instances in other parts of Ireland.

At sunrise a member of either the LDF (Local Defence Force) or LSF (Local Security Force) from Clonakilty, with perhaps a Garda Siochana, arrived in a small lorry. They had come to take these sailors or soldiers to the Curragh Camp where they would be interned until the war was over. They were happy as they left Joe's house. They gave us cigarette tobacco, much appreciated by my father, strange tasting white chocolate, and pemmican, a dried, powdered beef which also tasted strange. Joe gave us the paddle or oar which the men had used. I have it still.

This I will always remember: as they were walking towards the lorry a soldier noticed a young woman who had come from the village with the local men to see what 'was happening on the headland'. He gave a flirty skipping dance towards her and went away in the lorry. I never knew any of their names.

We went to school that morning with our friends and talked about all that had happened. In school Master Griffin asked me to stand up and tell him the story. I was completely tongue-tied and could only think he should be asking Michael, who was older than me and would know what to say. Somehow or other he got the information by question and answer and to my great relief that was the end of it. When we got home from school we were told more men from the same U-Boat had been picked up off the coast. Michael and I later found a small white silk parachute on the cliff. We decided it was from one of the flares.

The U-Boat is at the bottom of the sea. Divers have been down to explore the wreckage. All I can think of is how dark and eerie it must be to travel under the sea in a U-Boat.

Postscript[9]

Two months later the war in Europe ended. It had been going very badly for Germany towards the end. Were the men in the U-Boat aware of this? If they were seamen, and not soldiers as my father described them, they would have known they were in neutral Irish waters. Did they scuttle the vessel to avoid further involvement in the war?

On a small circle of paper in my mother's handwriting is the following:

'March 13th 1945 German crew ashore from U Boat. 11 in all'.

---

[9] Various other theories of what actually happened have surfaced over the years since. However, this was as Mary remembered it being talked of as a child.

Galley Head Lighthouse

Peggy

I was born at home in the 1940's assisted by the local doctor. My father was a Garda so we had a good standard of living and a comfortable house with a garden that provided much of our food needs. We had a vegetable plot, apple trees, a variety of fruit bushes, hens, turkeys for Christmas, and our own cow; all tended by our busy parents.

I was the youngest of nine children and my eldest sister was 14 years older than me. As soon as she got home from high school each day she was told, 'Get the child up and changed', and I was then her responsibility to mind. I went everywhere with her. Even when she was courting I was on the back of her bicycle when she and her boyfriend rode to Inchydoney Beach together. Eventually her wedding day arrived when I was 10 years old. It was a big shock to me to find I wasn't going on the honeymoon too! I just couldn't understand it.

My parents worked hard to ensure we all had a high school education. However, my father retired when I was ten, before we younger ones got through secondary school. My mother started up a bakery in a covered porch area at the back of our house, rising at 4am to make bread and cakes for the town in order to pay for our education, as secondary school was not free until 1966. My job was to deliver the finished goods to the shopkeepers during lunchtime. How I disliked that job! But, I am so grateful to my mother for the education I received.

I was reared with fear: fear of God and fear of authority, both at home and at school. Primary school was a happy time and I got on well there. But I didn't like secondary too much and there was huge fear there as well. If you did something wrong at school you got slapped and if your parents knew about it, you got slapped at home too.

The biggest highlight of summer was the Clonakilty Show. Crowds of people thronged down McCurtain Hill from the railway station through the town, to the Show Grounds, all generating a wonderful holiday atmosphere in the streets. My mother entered the Show cooking competitions and we were all pleased and proud of her, as she always did well in them.

There were loads of children in our street, so many that we had no need to go around the corner to make friends. We spent happy times playing 'Picky' (sometimes known as hop-scotch) with a stone and chalked lines on the street. We had skipping ropes and tops as well as playing tag.

When I was old enough to socialise at 17, we went to functions in the Industrial Hall. We were all expected to go straight home afterwards. However, there was always the temptation of having a quick cuddle with a favourite boy in a shop doorway en route. Woe betide those seen by the priest who never seemed to sleep at night. The congregation would be told at Sunday mass of the depravity of the young people in the town. The guilt if you knew he had identified you was enormous, even though he never said your name. So it was always a very short and nervous cuddle with one eye out for his approaching car.

After my father died when I was nineteen my mother gave me a small silver ring, very similar to a Claddagh ring, but without the crown above the heart. On the heart, held between two exquisitely made hands, were etched her initials. It was beautiful and finely made. She explained that my father had made it when he was a political prisoner on Spike Island, in Cork Harbour. Visitors used to smuggle small items into the prison in their shoes or socks. In this case a silver English sixpence had made its way to him and he had painstakingly fashioned it into this ring for his sweetheart. It was the first time I had seen the ring and heard its story. You can see the original sides of the sixpence on the inside of the ring.

McCurtain Hill

Hannah

A neighbour and midwife were in attendance at my premature birth at home in the late nineteen thirties. We lived three miles from the centre of town and walked to church and school, sometimes getting a lift in the neighbours horse and trap.

We didn't have umbrellas then. Our clothing consisted of coats, dresses, skirts and shoes or boots. The latter were obtained with assistance from a government subsidy that was available for the purchase of rough lace-up hobnail boots. Clothing and shoes were paid for weekly via account books at the drapers, with egg money from the hens. Schoolbooks were brought second hand, but we had new copy books.

We ate bread, butter and jam for lunch and for our dinner had vegetables with fry or stews, bacon or chicken. Milk puddings were made from bread and butter, rice or macaroni and we had blackberry, rhubarb or apple tarts all made by our mother. Hot cocoa drinks were a special treat. Our drinking water was drawn from the well.

We children helped out by the doing the washing up and small chores for our parents like going to town for messages, going for Woodbine cigarettes, taking the turkeys and goats to be mated, milking the goats, getting milk from our neighbour, catching the donkey for a trip to town, going to the river for a barrel of water for washing, taking the cart wheels to the river to tighten the rims, and picking blackberries and mushrooms.

For fun I played with my sister, my cousin and the neighbours. Favourite games were playing shops, climbing trees, blind man's bluff, rolling hoops (old bicycle wheels) and we had swings in the hay sheds. We went to the river to swim, paddle and catch fish in jam jars. Sometimes we went to the seaside on foot or in the donkey cart where we paddled and had picnics. Indoors we played cards and board games. We loved it when the Fun Fair came to town.

In the 1930's and 40's during the World War 2 years we had an aunt and cousins from England sheltering and sharing our house with us. Following primary school I attended Sacred Heart Secondary School[10] and left with my Leaving Certificate in the mid 1950's. Although Secondary education was not free in those days, there were allowances made for students from less affluent families and as long as you paid something, and did your best at school, you could continue your education.

My first job was in the Farm Products chicken hatchery on Casement St. They collected eggs from all the different breeds and after hatching, sold them as day old chicks. I think there could have been up to 30 people working there at any one time. Following that I worked for a short time relieving a sick teacher in the primary school. While my Leaving Cert. marks did not qualify me for entry to Teacher's Training College, I did do well enough to achieve the Junior Assistant Mistress qualification that was then part of the Leaving Certificate.

In 1958 three of us girls, left for England to begin our nursing training at Croyden. My sister was already there. Those years were a grand time for us all, as there were loads of Irish in London.

---

[10] Registered as Secondary School in 1941

Woodfield Days

Although I did not come to live in the Clonakilty area until 1974, we frequently had summer holidays with relatives at Woodfield in the early 1950's. I loved staying there, it was such a novelty to be without electricity and to draw water from a well. Never did water taste so good as that delicious well water. Going out into the fields each day was also pure pleasure.

Our Woodfield family grew linen flax, one of oldest crops still cultivated. Linen fabric has been made from flax since ancient times and the many by-products from its manufacture, such as seed, oil and tow, have been used in a multitude of ways over the centuries. It is a very labour intensive crop that called on every member of the family, plus the neighbours, to assist in many of the steps. In addition the women had to produce large quantities of food to nourish the workers. The production of linen in the West Cork area waxed and waned over the centuries due to economic factors. However World War 2 (1939-1945) shortages stimulated the industry again from 1941 to the mid 1950's.

The flax seed (linseed) was planted in the spring when the danger of frost had passed after preparing the soil in a way similar to that required if oats or barley were to be planted. After about three months growth, which included a period when its blue (or white) flowers bloomed, the flax was harvested. Before the linen seed was fully formed each plant had to be pulled up by the roots to avoid damaging the long flax fibres. They were then tied in bundles with binders made from specially prepared rushes. The next step involved the bundles of flax being immersed in carefully constructed ponds of water for some weeks to allow bacteria to assist in loosening the fibres from the stalks, a process called 'retting'. Retting was complete when the air was filled with an awful stench. The resulting product was then lifted out and spread over the fields to dry. This was back breaking, dirty and often painful work as the woody stems were rough and sharp. Depending on the weather, when dry, the flax would be loaded up and taken by horse and cart to the Flax Mill at Lisavaird for scutching, a process where machinery would break the woody stems to release the long linen fibres. Scutching by-products produced were tow (the short linen fibres) and the woody bits, which were called showells or shives. The clean fine linen fibre would be baled and taken to Clonakilty to be sold to the representatives of the linen mills in the north at the Flax Market.[11] The showells were a useful fuel source in times of shortage. However, my aunt used to pile them on top of the bastible when baking brown bread. She would light them and they quickly blazed up and died providing a short burst of heat to create a most delicious dark crust.When we visited the mill we children used to gather up any tow lying about and bring it home. There we would find an old bottle with a cork and jam the tow into the neck to make a doll with 'real' hair. The tow could hold in any number of fancy hairstyles and even be curled and keep its shape.

As well as happy memories, I also have a piece of history from Woodfield, a sampler that came to me as a grand-niece of General Michael Collins[12]. The sampler was stitched by his mother, Mary Anne O'Brien, and is believed to be on family produced linen. On the day that

---

[11] *For more information on linen production in West Cork see p.16 of The Ardfiedl/Rathbarry Journal 1998-99 for a detailed article by M Collins.*
[12] *The Irish revolutionary Leader, born at Woodfield 1890-1922.*

the British Army were burning down the family home, my Great Uncle, Liam Collins, was a baby who had been taken outside in his cradle. The soldiers snatched the cradle from the baby and flung it on the flames too. The sampler was one of the few things that survived the fire because it had been tied into a bundle and thrown from an upstairs window.

Years later the sampler went to my grandmother in Cork. My youngest aunt, Maeve, found it and had it framed. My grandmother wrote on the back of the sampler, 'For my daughter, Maeve'. Later when Maeve joined a religious order she gave it to me, adding another inscription on the back to that effect. So the back of the framed sampler has a written history all of its own.

Statue of General Michael Collins in Emmet Square, Clonakilty.

Child of the 1940's

Money was tight when we were children. We went to stay with more affluent relations in the summer, and they sent us back with their unwanted woollen coats. These would be taken to a dressmaker in Clonakilty who 'turned' them. In other words, remade them by putting the old outside on the inside, so that a brown coat with a red interior became a red coat with a brown interior. I was the last to get the big symbols of maturity then, nylons[13] and Cuban heels.

There was one very strict nun in the convent secondary school. If she deemed our knee-length skirts too short she would pin newspapers around the hem, which the unlucky girl had to wear for the day. Modesty was everything and to get pregnant was the biggest shame a girl could bring upon her family. She also told us, 'Even if a sperm lands on your knee, it can crawl up and get you pregnant'. The Catholic Church was totally in control of our lives. Its influence extended from the church to the schools and the health care system.

At home laundry was still done by hand in a wooden tub with a washboard and food was kept in a safe. This was a small cupboard on the outside of the house with mesh on two sides to let the breeze travel through. It was accessed from the inside of the house and provided a cool, vermin free place to store meat and other perishables for short periods. There were only about four streetlights in the town at the time. There was a wallpaper factory, which was a major employer in the town. Many people had wallpaper from the local factory on the walls of their homes. The more grand homes of the senior staff

---

[13] Suspender belts or garters held up nylon stockings. Or, in the absence of such items, by twisting the tops and tucking the twist in.

of the factory had quite an influence on the locals pride in their own dwellings and their aspirations.

A cinema in the town provided entertainment. It had a very long bench at the back where the courting couples used to sit. Lots of kissing used to go on there in that chaste era.

When I finished school I took up one of the few options allowing girls to move away from home and trained as a nurse. In the 1960's, when I was qualified and working on night shift, I saw my first condom. When patients were admitted via A & E their pockets were emptied and the contents checked and put in safe keeping. A condom had been found this way and it was sent the rounds of some of the nurses on night duty. What a talking point it provided as no one had seen one before, as contraception was not available in Ireland until the 1980's.

Washboard

A West Cork Farmer's Wife

I am a Kerry Woman and after leaving school in the early 1960's gained a clerical job in a bank. We worked from 9.30 am until 5 pm, although none could leave until the tellers had balanced the books, so occasionally it was later. In those times all the senior positions were held by men and there was no way that a woman could advance above the position of clerk, nor achieve a cashier's position, no matter how good she was at the job. There was also no chance of working in your own hometown, you were transferred to wherever you were needed entirely at the bank's discretion. We were all happy to accept this because in those days we felt very fortunate to have any job at all and a bank job was excellent because it was secure.

Catholic social teaching, based on the belief that a woman's 'natural role' was as a wife and mother, heavily influenced early Government thinking. Women were expected to be 'modest, retiring and obedient'. In addition it was considered that working women were taking jobs from men with families to keep. This resulted in the introduction of the 1932 Public Service Marriage Bar[14]. Originally brought in to cover teachers, it spread to nurses and many other occupations. While working in the bank in I met my future husband and on our marriage in 1967, I was thus dismissed from the bank and began my new role as a farmer's wife in the Clonakilty area.

In the late 1960's there were substantial numbers of educated women attracted to farm life. Agriculture was in an expansionist mode and farmers were doing well financially. The effect of rural electrification was starting

---

[14] *The Marriage Bar was withdrawn in 1972. However, for teachers it was lifted in 1957.*

to bring prosperity to the faming community through the use of milking machines and water pumps. Wives could see an outlet for the skills they had gained in their working lives, for example, through keeping the farm accounts. Often the business focus they brought to the job was an advantage to the profit side of farming. The women worked hard for the farm, doing all the cooking every day, feeding extra workers at harvest time, being available at a moment's notice to provide an extra pair of hands to assist with everyday farming tasks, as well as bringing up children and ensuring that they received a good education, plus keeping a good home.

However, due to the male focus on men's work being more important in those times, the PRSI contributions of the women were overlooked when many farmers and their accountants paid tax for future pensions. Thus many women, now in their early 70's, after decades of record keeping and helping out with farm work, had to fight for the right to a state pension because the government had no record of them working for the minimum period required. A famous letter from a farm wife in the Farmer's Journal at the time stated that, 'she, along with doing all the other jobs on the farm, had to stand in for Shep [15], when Shep was missing!' However, some accountants did pay the PRSI contribution as the wives were legally deemed to be partners in work and ownership.

The first time I stayed in the home of my future in-laws was after I became engaged. As I had been transferred miles from Co. Cork north with the bank, if I wanted to see my boyfriend, I had to stay with his cousins nearby. My mother and father-in-law, as was the common rural

---

[15] The dog.

custom, then lived with us for the first decade or more of our marriage. They had been late marrying, as they had to wait until the Civil War of 1922-1923 was over, because they had been on different sides. The history of 600 years of English oppression, the War of Independence from 1919-1921 and the Civil War has had a huge impact on the psyche of the Irish people. People became very cute (cagey) and kept their business and thoughts to themselves. This persisted until fairly recent times with, for example, farmers keeping their acreage, and stock numbers closely guarded.

Another huge historic impact on the fortunes of the agricultural community was known as the Economic War, or Anglo-Irish Trade War, which came after the fight for freedom and Civil war and lasted from 1932 until 1938. It came about because De Valera's government refused to honour provisions made in the 1921 Anglo-Irish Treaty for land annuities to be paid to Britain[16]. The result was a protectionist trade war with unilateral trade barriers imposed by both sides that resulted in Irish farmers losing the market for much of their production. The knock-on effects were severe social suffering and financial loss for Ireland. Eventually measures were instituted to offset this, such as making Irish Cattle and British Coal cheaper and easier to purchase, and this eventually gave rise to the Anglo-Irish Trade agreement that effectively brought about the end of the trade war three years later. However, these extremely difficult times left a long legacy of deprivation, for farmers and their families in particular, to cope with.

---

[16] The Irish Lands Act 1870 had enabled some Irish tenant farmers to buy their own lands with the help of British loans, which were to be repaid by annuities.

Macra na Feirme, a network of clubs was founded in 1944 by a group of 12 agricultural advisors, rural science teachers and farmers with the aim of helping the personal development of young rural people. It provides training and experience in many aspects of farming, communication and social abilities and has since made a big contribution to country life for those aged between 17 and 35, both male and female.

I think that Mary Robinson[17], our first female President of Ireland from 1990 to 1997 was also a huge positive influence for the women of Ireland. As a strong independent woman, an academic and barrister, combined with good looks, a husband and family she drew a large following with her championing of women's rights.

Former Taoiseach[18] Charles Haughey, although now a controversial figure, in the course of his long career also brought about beneficial changes to the laws affecting women, such as: family planning, legitimacy of children, discrimination against women in inheritance rights, free secondary education and also put in place free transport and electricity for old age pensioners. He also effectively abolished the death penalty and supported the arts by giving tax free status to writers and artists and making books VAT free.

---

[17] Elected directly by the people she served two seven year terms in the largely ceremonial role before going on to become United Nations High Commissioner for Human Rights.
[18] Prime Minister

An Educator

One of my early memories of Clonakilty as a child in the 1950's, was staying with my uncle a priest, in Emmet Square on New Year's Eve. In bed at midnight I was startled to hear a loud bell ringing outside the window. Looking into the deserted Emmet Square I saw a man on the back of a lorry ringing a hand bell while being driven from street to street in the town to announce the New Year to everyone. It was so different from the celebrations of today.

My father was a hard working, self-educated farmer who believed in the importance of a good education for all of his seven children. That is how I came to board in the Sacred Heart Secondary School in Clonakilty in the mid 1960's.

It was a tough regime in those days. School was based on the male model of control in society. We had to eat our breakfast in silence, as if silence would stop us thinking or interacting. We only went home for the school holidays. The rest of the time we were within the confines of the school save for walking to confession at the parish church on Saturdays and on Sundays going on long supervised exercise walks. Our lives were dominated by schoolwork, which embraced Saturday morning as well. In the evenings we studied from 5pm to 7pm and broke for supper, then studied again from 7.30pm to 9.30pm, or 10pm, if important exams were looming. Sport and exercise were not catered for in a big way. We played netball amongst ourselves, and tennis if we were interested and had a racquet.

The lights went out at 10pm but most of us had torches. I ruined my eyesight reading under the blankets until all hours. It was a sad day when the batteries ran out because we Boarding School girls were forbidden from entering any of the shops in town and could not replace them until the holidays. There was a little sweet shop on Ashe Street that had a jukebox. We gave our town dwelling classmates money to play popular songs for us as we dawdled past on our way to confession and when we lingered outside on our way back. It was magic to hear Elvis, the Beatles or the Capital Showband this way.

On Sundays we also wrote home to our parents who received the letter the following Tuesday. Our reply came the following Friday. It was by letter from school that I told my parents that I had decided on the life of a religious sister. It seemed a long wait to hear their response. Both were happy and not so happy about my decision, but they supported me in my choice. Most girls then went from school at 17 or 18 to begin their novitiate. At that time anyone who wanted to become a nun could do so without a dowry needing to be paid.

It was a frugal life, but times in general were hard. Until the mid 1970's the hooded West Cork cloak was still occasionally seen being worn on the streets of Clonakilty and there were people in Clonakilty still suffering from want. The nuns delivered many helpful baskets of food to needy households on Sunday after lunch. We nuns still wore our long black serge habits even when I was with students who played in the volleyball championships in Bristol in 1980. The habit finally changed to short dresses and veils in the 1990's and the wearing of them is now optional.

Once I had taken my orders I trained as a teacher of Home Economics. The choice of training was decided by the needs of the time and for the good of the school. Our teaching salaries were paid into the religious community fund for the upkeep of all the community. At the time, a portion of the salary of any sister teaching science was put into a special fund that was used in the school to encourage the teaching of science subjects to girls and to provide facilities that were not grant aided.

As a teacher, over time I have noticed changes in the expectations of the parents of our pupils. Earlier in my career the majority of parents turned up to the school parent/teacher evenings and were deeply interested in who their child was becoming. In later years fewer parents came but the focus became more sharply upon the results their child was achieving. The teaching of skills rather than knowledge has become downgraded and is no longer valued in the urge to have every child going on to college, whether they are suited to it or not.

So Sacred Heart Secondary school formed a bigger part of my life than I ever dreamed it would when I first unpacked my belongings there. It was the dominant part of it for almost 40 years. It formed me into who I am. The interaction with students, teachers, parents and the wider community was enriching. It is such a vibrant and caring community to work in and with – community being the important word. There is a sense of pride and care that is tangible.

A Former Pupil

I was fourteen when my sister and I came to live in Clonakilty as Sacred Heart Secondary School (SHSS) pupils and residents of the Mary Immaculate Boarding School on Mt Carmel. There were 58 other pupils in the boarding facility, which had only been in existence for two years.

We lived on the top floor of the school and in the 1960's students who were sisters were housed in a separate dormitory. Very small cubicles were screened from each other by an arrangement of curtains and partial walls. Each contained a double bed that we shared and lockers for our indoor clothing. All the boarders were locked in at night with a nun sleeping on the same floor. In retrospect, it seemed like a big fire risk and I never remember taking part in a fire drill.

Our days began when a nun ringing a bell arrived at our cubicle with a cup of holy water that was thrust through the curtains. As each of us took the water to bless ourselves, she would know we were out of bed. We each fetched cold water from the only tap on the floor in our basins and washed before daily Mass at 8am. After Mass we ate a good breakfast in the refectory. I remember delicious brown bread, butter, boiled eggs, and cornflakes. Some of the girls did not like the boiled eggs and would stuff them into their gym tunics to pass on to the day pupils to dispose of. We could each bring our own supply of jam. I cherished a jar of lemon curd as an absolute luxury if I was ever lucky enough to have one. Once breakfast was over we had jobs to do, clearing tables, washing up, drying and polishing until the school day began at 9am.

Tuition fees were due for all secondary pupils until 1966 when free secondary education was introduced in Ireland. Until then the Fees at SHSS began at £6 per pupil, increasing annually to £12. Science was not part of the curriculum for girls until 1964.

At midday we had dinner and then tea when classes finished at 3.30pm. Homework was supervised before and after supper at 7.30pm. Before bed at 10pm there was also a recreation period where we would do drill and pastimes such as Irish dancing. The school library also provided some diversion. Of course, we did not always lie down like good girls and sleep after lights out. We threw back the curtains and had loads of fun talking and laughing quietly.

Baths were taken weekly on a rota basis. Our modesty was preserved there by privacy, but how mortifyingly embarrassed we were if we got sick and Dr Collins was called, because we had to pull up our vests for him to examine our chests. However, if we were sick in bed we were always given the treat of a hot orange cordial drink and an apple at 4pm.

On Saturday mornings we had classes as well, and later our chores to do, cleaning out our lockers, polishing shoes. We were never allowed outside the school unless supervised and would all be taken in to town to confession at the church there. On Sunday mornings we dressed in our Sunday uniform to go to church, and as we hardly saw a young male from one week's end to the next, we all had crushes (unrequited of course) on the altar boys. In the afternoons we would go in procession on supervised walks, sometimes in the countryside to Inchydoney Island, or Ballinascarthy.

Some of the girls were lucky enough to have visits from family and friends, but we did not. I was four years in the Boarding School where we stayed with the exception of school holidays. After we gained our Leaving Certificate results we were all called to the Principal's office and asked if we had any leanings toward religious life. I did not and left to train as a nurse. I would have preferred to go to university and work with numbers, but nursing was one of the few ways of gaining a qualification with accommodation supplied while in paid employment.

Overall, I felt very fortunate during my school days. The nuns were good to me. Despite the narrow confines of life at boarding school, I was well looked after, gained a good education and made lifelong friends.

Requirements for Boarders in 1960[19]
1 navy coat & beret
1 dark bottle-green gym, tunic
1 dark fir-green round neck jumper without collar
1 dark fir-green cardigan
2 white blouses with long sleeves and shirt collar
3 coat hangers and 1 skirt hanger
1 pair light indoor shoes – brown
1 dressing gown and 1 pair of bedroom slippers
2 nightdresses or pyjamas
2 sets usual underclothing
1 green coat overall long sleeves
2 pairs blankets and 1 rug, 2 pairs sheets, 2 bolster cases
3 toilet towels, usual toilet requisites, sufficient stockings
2 knives, 2 forks, 3 spoons tea, soup, dessert) marked with initials
tennis racket and shoes
Sunday uniform – skirt, blouse, blazer, scarf and beret
All these items must be clearly marked with the boarder's full name
Birth certificate, Boarding fee: £55.00 per year (laundry included) £100 for two sisters. Payable half yearly in September and February. Drill: 15/- per year
Music: 25/- per term extra

---

[19] List taken from the SHSS Golden Jubilee Year Book 1991

Dena O'Donovan

Although my twin brother and I lived with our family in Cork, every weekend and school holidays were spent in Clonakilty. There were seven children in my family but we two spent more time than the others at the family hotel, O'Donovan's. My earliest memory is of my brother driving his Dinky toy cars around the green swirls of the carpet pattern in the Drawing Room there. In the mid 1960's, from about the age of nine to eleven, my brother and I had jobs; sheet folding, bottle sorting and polishing glasses. There was a house laundry on site and as we got older I was also entrusted with ironing.

The large function room now known as 'The Venue' used to be known as the 'The Dancehall'. It was the big band era and there was much entertainment each Saturday night with entertainers like Dicky Rock and local bands playing. There was very little alcohol consumed at such functions then, mainly soft drinks like Deasy's Orange and Cidona. Men and women sat in chairs lining each side of the dancehall, men on one side, women on the other. The chairs had legs made of tubular metal and our job was to crawl forward along the tunnel made by the chair legs, where people might be seated, and retrieve the empty glasses. We did this by crawling out again backwards as soon as we had enough to carry in our two hands, and then repeating the process all over again.

The Hotel was then a 'commercial hotel' designed to assist the many travelling sales and business people. There were ten guest bedrooms, and ten identically numbered desks with a lamp and papers for business use in 'The Commercial Room'. There were ten corresponding tables in the dining room. The bar tender looked after reception as well, and also sold BP petrol from a bowser out the front. When the first TV arrived ten armchairs were arrayed around it, in what is now known as the Green Room. The bar was the place for men to drink while couples or ladies were served in the Hotel Lounge Bar at the back of the house. They paid a penny more for the privilege of taking a drink there rather than in the front bar.

One of the distinctive women associated with the hotel was 'Miss Katty' or 'Aunty Kat', pictured above. Catherine O'Donovan was born in 1882. Never marrying, she ran the hotel herself from 1918 and rode to the hunt with Castletownshend authors Somerville and Ross as well as Lord Carbery from Castlefreke. She wore trousers, was one of the first females in Ireland to abandon the side-saddle when riding horseback, and smoked in public. Over time she also reared several children from the extended family under her roof in the hotel and had 22 godchildren some of whom are still living. Aunty Kat and my great grandfather were two of a family of 18 children, many of whom emigrated to the US or Canada. When Aunty Kat returned from one of her extensive travels to visit her siblings she brought back a child whom she claimed was her sister's. However, it was believed by many locally to be her own son. Later as an adult, he came from America to live with her for a time, but it will never be known for sure if the relationship was so, as he sadly died prematurely from pneumonia while travelling just nine days after his marriage. Damp hotel beds were blamed for his sad demise.

Before Aunty Kat died she sold the hotel at a nominal rate to her grandnephew, our father Thomas, to avoid disagreements over succession. He was the only family member in the locality that had shown an interest in the hotel. Looked after by our father, Aunty Kat lived on in one of the rooms at the hotel until her death in 1954. After she passed away we heard stories of her quiet kindness to some of the more hard-up local families through her distribution of food from the hotel back door.

I attended St Angela's, the Urseline Convent school in Cork and after leaving went to Lee Commercial College for a year. Following that I studied architectural draughtsmanship and town planning at CIT, then worked in architectural offices for a decade. I spent three years of that, after my father died, in Sydney. My sister Ann had emigrated there as a teacher, taking up an assisted £10.00 passage. Meanwhile, brother Tom had studied hotel management and took over running the hotel. I returned to Clonakilty to assist him around 1987.

At that time socialising in pubs was very much a male thing and usually only one or two women would make up the throng in the bar. I remember feeling very daunted standing behind the semi-circular bar of the time and having people two or three rows deep all focusing on me. Having to speak up loud and call out 'time' was nerve wracking until I lost my shyness after a few weeks. Then, it was considered somewhat unseemly for women to drink beer. How times have changed. Now the bar usually has more women than men, all socialising in groups, and it is nothing to be serving them pints.

O'Donovan's Hotel has now been run by the same family for over 200 years, one of the longest in Ireland and is the hub of the town. Cosy bar fireplace pictured below.

Growing up in Rural West Cork in the Nineteen Twenties
By Margaret Feen

This original life story was beautifully hand written on unlined foolscap paper by Margaret Feen, mostly in the 1980's. In 2012 she generously and spontaneously gave it to me, as an unpublished document, to use in my project. I subsequently talked with Margaret on a number of occasions and have added additional information and explanations gained in italics or footnotes. In addition I have included a short true story she had written for the Ardfield Rathbarry Journal.

Margaret is an exceptional woman, with a wonderful intellect and excellent recall. I love her writing style for its simple clarity of expression and celebration of all the best things in life: the beauty of nature, the satisfaction of hard work well done and the joy in simple pleasures. As a long term computer user I can only marvel at her immaculate pages of perfect prose. While she has been confined to her home for some years now, at 94, she still has a very sharp mind and excellent recall. I think her memories will bring much pleasure to you, whether you are a local person, someone with an interest in the locality of Clonakilty, or some one like me from a different world altogether.

Forward by Margaret Feen

Women's role in the 1920's, when I was growing up, was only a degree above slavery (and I presume it was a little better than in the preceding generation). Men were lords and masters and ruled over their women with a rod of iron. The main feature of the times was a lack of respect which showed in the huge families the women had to produce and care for in the most primitive conditions. Ireland then was mostly a land of small (very) farms.

Previously, after years of possession by a neighbouring country, settlers were brought in and given all the good land, leaving very stony, poor unproductive little lots for the natives.

Women along with producing a baby a year, had to help the men to break up the land to put potatoes in. Potatoes were the staple food. Indeed I am sure that many Irish children never tasted any other kind of food if the money wasn't there to buy flour. Mothers went without in order to put a bit of food in their children's mouths. After the dreadful Famine, which devastated the country, the population was halved. Political figures started to get active and after another long struggle the landlords began renting some of their estates. People got more independent and were able to grow crops to support themselves.

I remember my own mother, the former Kate Hurley, (pictured) and how hard she worked to rear seven of us on a small farm. Her work was made harder because my father was an invalid as a result of injury to his spinal cord. She was out in the morning at six o'clock to bring in the seven cows and milked them before my brothers were old enough to help. Food had to be prepared and fed to calves and pigs, poultry seen to, and all this before she called us for school. The fire had to be cleaned of ashes and got going with the kettle for the breakfast hanging over it to boil. We had tea and brown bread for breakfast, brown bread and a bottle of milk in our school bags for lunch. She had to go to the field to dig potatoes for the dinner, cook the (seldom) bit of bacon and vegetables to feed us all on our return from school, prepare for the evening chores and see that the animals were bedded then come in and help prepare the tea. This would be a typical day's work for most women along with the tub of washing, the mending and the darning, and making clothes for the family. Along with all that there was the farm work where she had to help, setting the potatoes in the spring, saving the harvest, and feeding hungry men. Everything that happened inside and out, the men expected the women to help. There was so much truth in the old saying, 'A woman's work is never done.'

Technology and progress changed the face of women's labour but we must always remember the huge debt we owe them.

Emigration too made a big difference. Where with great difficulty, the fare to America was gathered for the first of the family, after a few years she was able to send for the next one and so on. What those brave girls went through alone in a strange land and having to adapt to city life and a totally new culture, and often managing to send a few dollars home to relieve the misery.

My Own Place

Looking back over the years and the decades it seems that I've been around a very long time. Ardfield, my native parish lies to the south of Clonakilty, a parish of headlands washed by the Atlantic, and a coastline dotted with ruined castles built by the land owning class. The district too had its quota of 'big houses': Boss Croker of Tammany Hall fame, the Hungerfords, Beamishes, Galweys – dwindling relics of the old landlord system.

The early twenties was an era of intense class distinction. The gentry still owned a big share of the land even though this stranglehold was broken by the land agitation under Parnell[20] and Davitt[21] while the farmers and cottiers [22] fiercely held on to their precious and hardly won acres.

Home for me, Dunnycove, was a small farm of reasonably good land and a typical West Cork farmhouse with traditional roses round the door. My mother had 'green fingers' and she had a magnificent sweet smelling 'Constance Spry' type of rose trailing round the door. Even the most sophisticated modern breeders could never surpass the heady perfume of that beautiful rose.

I was the youngest of six children with two sisters who had emigrated to Boston and three brothers. Our family life was different from our neighbours owing to the fact that my father was an invalid for as long as I can remember – crippled from the waist as a result of an accident. In those far off days there were neither operations, drugs nor injections and I can remember

---

[20] Charles Stewart Parnell 1846-1891
[21] Michael Davitt 1846-1906
[22] A labourer renting a small portion of land at a rent fixed by competition.

vividly his intense suffering, but his innate good humour. His courage and faith kept him going and made him an inspiration to everybody round him.

My birth coincided with the birth period of our Free State and I grew up with the 'Young Ireland'. Being born in the early twenties meant growing up in an intensely active political scene, and in spite of the fact that we lived at the extreme end of the country there was a very keen awareness of what was happening nationally. In my own family this interest was accentuated by the fact that my father was a near relation of O'Donovan Rossa's[23] and Michael Collins was born a few miles away in the next parish. Our only contact with the outside world was the 'Cork Examiner' and even though it only cost 2 old pence very few people could afford it daily. The 'Southern Star', while keeping its 'eye on Russia' supplied us with all the local news.

School Days

Strangely enough I can't remember my first day at school. Having no sister I was taken care of by my neighbour's daughter, a kind sensitive girl, Mary Esther. The School was a two roomed building, cold and draughty with a fire at one end – unfortunately not ours. In the very cold weather we had turns warming our hands a few times a day. There were two teachers one of whom taught the infants, first and second classes, the other teacher had the third, fourth, fifth, sixth and seventh, about 80 pupils altogether. School in the twenties was so different from modern times. We learned everything off by heart – poetry, spelling, grammar, tables, history, geography and catechism. We learned to

---

[23] Jeremiah O'Donovan Rossa 1831-1915

write by using headlines, and with the aid of charts we identified everyday objects and learned how to put sentences together. As we progressed to the higher classes we had reading and spelling sessions and tried to grasp the intricacies of grammar and punctuation. The school programme, in retrospect, was a very comprehensive one and we had needlework twice a week and nature study. There was often a jar of frogs' spawn at the window, and we observed their progress and imbibed the rudiments of biology from plant life. It was a very crowded schedule and the teacher had to have five different programmes going, to cater for classes from third to seventh. Overcrowding was an unknown term and at that time no child left school before 14 years at the earliest.

There were no school meals in the days of my youth. We walked the miles on a breakfast of tea and brown home-made bread and brought two slices of bread and butter and a bottle of milk for lunch, which we ate out in the yard on fine days and in bad weather we dined in the classroom – the second room in the school which acted as cloak room and general utility.

The standard of hygiene was primitive. The only pretence of washing facilities was a wash stand and basin and a bucket of cold water brought from a nearby well each morning, but we were hale and healthy and didn't know the meaning of the word 'germs' which no doubt abounded in our antiquated dry toilets.

Our teachers were very hard working and dedicated, working under extreme handicaps to instil knowledge into unreceptive young minds. Indeed they acted as nursemaids as well as teachers and always saw that the less well off never went without a lunch. Even though corporal punishment was part of school life the stick was seldom used, the threat of it acted satisfactorily. In those young carefree days we did not always appreciate the lessons we learnt and the religious foundation established by our teachers and we owe them a big debt of gratitude for their unselfish efforts on our behalf.

Photograph

This photograph of my brother and me was taken in the nineteen twenties when I was about ten years old. My sister was visiting and she posed us outside our Dunnycove farmhouse and had a coloured photograph made when she went back home to Boston.

I was always the best-dressed girl in school as my clothes were all hand-me-downs from a well off cousin in Dunmanway. As I was the youngest child in the family my mother also had time to make things for me, either knitted or crocheted. I well remember the lovely collar, bonnet and gloves she made me from navy blue wool with a band of white fur around the face, neck and wrists. Being the youngest child was a privileged place to be. However, it was a disadvantage when it came to caring for babies and children, as I knew nothing of them until I had my own. Our farmhouse was a typical one of the times, with two rooms downstairs and three rooms upstairs. You entered the house via the kitchen, which had the stairs to the bedrooms on one side, and the kitchen led into the sitting room. The outhouses were to the side of the house.

Heart of the Home

The kitchen was the centre of activity in every farm home. It was usually the biggest room in the house with an 'open' fireplace and a fire machine [24], the wheel of which had to be turned by hand to create a good draught. The settle provided seating accommodation, and the big table and chairs were white wood and were taken outside on Saturday and scrubbed with sand. No comfort as regards flooring – the floor was cement and my mother scrubbed that too on Saturday night. A big cupboard held all the foodstuffs and, on the top shelf, the clothes that were needed from day to day. But the pride and joy of every country woman's heart was the dresser. It was indeed 'filled with shining delph speckled and white and blue

---

[24] A type of bellows.

and brown'[25]. On our dresser there was a collection of Blue and Brown Willow, from the big meal dishes down to the teacups, jugs of all sizes, lovely lustre and floral patterns and rows of coloured basins. An average dresser would have at least 100 pieces and it was a major job taking them down and washing them and putting them back shining. The parlour was little used except maybe at Christmas and Stations time.

In every farm house there was a dairy or cool room. Those were for creamery days: Sir Horace Plunkett's co-operative movement had not yet reached West Cork. The milk was kept in big earthenware pans, having been strained and left to set. Once a week (or twice in summer) the cream was skimmed off and butter made in the churn. It was then washed well and wrapped in white cloths (flour bags) and sold in the local shop. My mother washed and boiled the flour bags and bleached them on the grass until they were as white as snow. They were used as sheets and pillowcases and of course tea cloths. A very versatile article the big hundredweight flour bag and it was possible then to buy them so cheaply in flourmills.

Washing was another big chore and the age of synthetics and other easily washed clothing wasn't even a dream at that stage. All the underclothes were heavy, the men usually wore flannel and the working shirts were strong and hard to wash. The water had to be boiled in the big iron pot and the clothes soaped on the table and scrubbed on the washboard. Anything boilable was boiled in the pot. The Sunday shirts were white and the

---

[25] China or crockery. Quote from the poem 'An Old Woman of the Roads' by Padraic Colum,

men wore starched collars and fronts. It was possible to buy these detached. My mother ironed with a box iron. She put the heaters into the fire until they glowed red and then, with the poker took them out, put them into the iron, closed the little doors and ironed away on the kitchen table. On the starched collars she used a special small glossing iron and rubbed away until they shone. When some years later we got a range it changed the atmosphere of the kitchen. The open fire and fire machine were transferred to the 'back kitchen' and most of the work was done there.

There was bread baked every day: big bastible cakes of brown flour milled from our own wheat. The bastible was heated over the flames and the cover 'reddened' on the coals. When the cake was put into the red hot bastible, the cover was put on again with the poker, and the red coals put on top. Timing was incidental – according to the heat of the fire. Some people who could not afford coal or turf collected the dried cow pats. It burned quite well but you would get the smell a mile away!

Entertainment

Growing up in an era of great political activity we learned and sang mostly patriotic songs both at school and at home. Young people today would find it impossible to visualise life without radio, TV and other technology, but that precisely was the situation. My sister on a visit home from Boston brought a gramophone and what a novelty it was. It was played so often that the records were worn out in a short time. Our nearest neighbour's son was a radio officer on a ship and brought home a battery operated radio. That was the eighth wonder of the world and we could not figure out the intricacies of it. The batteries had to be charged at regular intervals in a garage and we were able to hear (with luck) the news and the matches from Croke Park. There was always an overflow audience on such occasions.

People in the country created their own amusement in those days and in our house we had a ceilidhe[26] every Sunday night. The kitchen table was put outside and my father played the melodeon[27] and twenty or more young and not so young people danced the sets, waltzes, military two steps, long and short schottise, Walls of Limerick and Bridge of Athlone. Most of the young people of the area learned to dance on our kitchen floor. Everything started early and ten o'clock was the deadline as everybody had to be home by ten thirty.

Again probably because my father was an invalid, we always had neighbours in at night 'scoraiochting'[28] and many a hair raising ghost story was told around the big fire of wood. The old people excelled at story telling and most of them believed in or had a healthy respect for the 'little folk'. I often sat frozen in my seat under the chimney listening to the tales of the witchery of the 'Sprid a Camus' who intercepted any traveller who had occasion to be out before cock-crow, and 'Crapa leasa' who allegedly roamed the graveyards with chains dangling. Later though we found out that the chains turned out to be the tying on Tim Jack's donkey's legs, which lived in the field adjacent to the graveyard.

All the happenings of the parish and beyond were discussed at that fireside. My father read anything interesting out of the paper, and when we only got the odd paper everything was of interest. When my mother

---

[26] A social event with traditional, singing dancing and story telling.
[27] A small accordion
[28] Story telling

went to town we got 'Our Boys' or maybe 'Ireland's Own'. We were lucky in as far as reading was concerned in that a cousin in Kildare who was involved in horses sent my father a parcel of books regularly. By the time I reached ten years I had read more of Nat Gould's books than any punter in the Curragh and I was in on any elusive movement of the Scarlet Pimpernel. At Christmas there were always 'Girls Annual' in the parcel: what a lovely treat they were and I shared them with my best friends.

I never remember a pair of shop socks coming into our house in my young days. My mother knitted all the socks for my father and brothers. Indeed I can truly say her hands were never idle. She made quilts with little baubles of white cotton thread, she covered old blankets with cotton cretonne, she made crochet shawls and bonnets. All that as well as mending and darning the heavy working clothes at the end of a heavy day's work in the indifferent light of the lamp on the wall.

Meitheal Memories[29]

Looking back to those far off days it was a miracle how people got through so much work with so few conveniences. Starting at about 6am in summer the cows had to be brought in and milked, the milk strained and put to set in the dairy, and the cows and pigs fed and we always had a few little ones which needed constant attention. Owing to my father's health problem my mother had much extra work and while my brothers were young she had to work on the land as well. There were potatoes to be put in as well as having to cut the scillauns

---

[29] A group, often of neighbours, gathered together to perform a task, with some social element added.

[30], hay to be saved and the harvest was an exceptionally busy time. Hay saving we loved. It was a pleasant task to turn the rows of newly mown sweet smelling hay and make it up into small cocks which were later made into big ones. The cocks were brought into the haggard in an operation known as 'slinging'. It was done by encircling the cocks with a strong rope which was attached to the horse, and many the tumble we got off the cocks when we were let ride on them. But it was all glorious fun and the loveliest part of all was the tea in the hayfield. My mother brought out a sweet-tin [31] of strong hot tea and currant cake and no Cordon Bleu Cuisine could ever taste as good as that feast on a lovely June day.

Maybe nostalgia makes everything seem rosy, but I am sure that it was a fact that in the 1920's and 1930's the seasons came in their proper times and from May to September there was very little rain and the long hot summers made the work of saving the harvest much easier. I can't help thinking how much today's children are missing out on. Silage harvesters have taken all the fun out of hay making. No longer is the big thatched rick in the haggard. Mechanisation has changed the whole leisurely farming scene to one of big noisy machines, smelly silage and impersonality.

When the hay was safe in the haggard and the rick snugly thatched the corn was ripening and the biggest task of the year was upon us – the cutting and harvesting of the grain. The corn was cut with a mowing machine drawn by two horses but I can remember seeing scythes being used and even hooks in very small areas. The children usually got the task of 'picking the sops' –

---

[30] Seed potatoes.
[31] A recycled tin from a sweet shop, with a lid and wire handle.

gathering the stray straws after the sheaves were bound. The sheaves were then stooked, four in each side with heads meeting and with room to let the wind through to dry them well. The next stage of stacking needed a big effort and it was the children's job to draw the stooks together for hand stacks. These, after a few days drying in the sun, were brought into the haggard to await the coming of the threshing engine.

Threshing was 'D' day and because it happened in September we had the added bonus of a holiday from school. I can remember the horse driven thresher where four horses were driven round a circular area. They rotated an axle like piece of machinery, which connected by belts, drove the drum – the machine which separated the grain from the straw. This was where the meitheal gathered. All the neighbouring farmers 'cored', that is, helped one another. Each man had his own task – picking sheaves off the stacks, cutting binders, feeding the sheaves into the drum, picking the straw out on one side and collecting the grain into sacks on the other side, winnowing, which meant separating the grain from the chaff in a hand operated machine, and of course making the rick.

Rick-making was a highly specialised craft and certain men in each area were in great demand for this important task. The layers of straw were laid and packed well and the top shaped in roof form and thatched to withstand the wind and rain. Straw proved good feeding for cattle along with the hay and it was very important to have it well protected. Sugans[32] were made to tie down the rick and weighted with heavy stones. It could be sliced like a loaf of bread in the late autumn and winter.

---

[32] Straw ropes

The hustle and bustle of threshing day had to be seen to be understood. In the 1930's the horse work outfit was replaced with the petrol engine and later, the progression to the big steam engine took place. The demise of the meitheal came with the combine harvester and a completely new scene emerged in Irish farming, leaving the excitement and activity of threshing time only a memory.

The harvest was a time of plenty for man and beast. All the farmers grew wheat, oats and barley. The wheat was carefully stored in the loft for flour for the household. There were oats for the horses and barley was sold either to the milling companies in the town, or in the case of malting barley, it was sold to the brewery in Bandon for the production of whiskey.

Threshing day was one of intense activity for us children. We helped our mother to prepare food for the 30 or more hungry men, a herculean task and we had to collect extra cutlery and crockery from the neighbours. There were huge pots of potatoes, bacon and cabbage cooked and several very large currant cakes baked the day before as well as the mountain of shop-bread. It was all back-breaking work but so satisfying, and tired as everybody was, there was always 'a night' singing and dancing and the older men drinking porter, the younger ones got lemonade. The neighbours who did not have land to grow corn collected big bags of chaff, which they used to make mattresses. These and feather ticks were in use everywhere and it was quite some time later that the hair and fibre mattresses came into vogue.

When the corn was sold, all the bills incurred in the production: seed, manure, threshing costs etc. were paid and clothes and shoes purchased for the winter. The harvest was a happy rewarding time when the results of hard physical labour were brought to fruition. The farmers were able to balance their budgets and face the winter secure in the knowledge that their families and livestock were provided for the in the barns and the haggards[33].

In my rather long lifetime, nothing has changed more drastically than the Irish farming scene. I am thinking particularly of the dairying area and of cows – their hugely increased numbers and the unbelievably progressive methods of their care and maintenance.

Away back in the 1920's when I was growing up, the cows were then, as now, the mainstay of every farming family and were treated with respect and almost devotion. Young progressive farmers would find it hard to envisage the old type stall where the cows lived in comfort during the long winter months bedded in a thick layer of straw. Very few farmers had more than 10 cows, intimately known by individual names – Rosie, Daisy, Strawberry etc., and each animal had an identity with the regular milker. Women were considered to be better and more patient milkers and when a cow was restive – maybe with a sore teat- she responded to the soothing voice of the cailin[34] singing or talking to her, like, 'Yeossh Rosie, easy girl'. Heifers invariably had to be spancelled[35] for their first milking and the milker was often in a vulnerable position when a kick could land herself and the bucket in the passageway.

---

[33] Area of ground close to the house and barn where the hay shed and corn ricks were.
[34] Young girl
[35] Hind legs tied with rope

This was all so long ago, before electricity and milking machines were even a dream. Sir Horace Plunkett eased a lot of the hard work when he brought the Co-operative[36] movement and the creameries to every part of the country.

The last chore in the winter nights was to light the storm lantern and 'go out to see the cows and horses'. The warmth and comfort of the stall with contented animals munching sweet smelling hay laced with sliced turnips was probably too conducive to TB germs, but what comfort they lived in compared to the modern open yards. But that I suppose is progress. It has wiped out so many of the old customs like burning the udder hair off the newly calved cows and blessing them with the blessed candle and holy water. Another era, other traditions: who is to say that it wasn't a better life for man and beasts.

Summer jobs

The summer job is no new phenomenon and the six weeks break from school meant that there were plenty of jobs lined up for us on the farm. The harvest time we loved, but there were other less pleasant tasks. Thinning turnips and mangolds was hot work on a July day and the knees and fingers suffered from contact with the rough, dry earth. One chore that had to be done regardless was drawing water. Many young people nowadays would find it hard to realize that water did not always come at the turn of a tap, but in the parish where I grew up, the long hot summers were synonymous with water shortage. Most people relied on wells three or four feet deep that

---

[36] *The Lisavaird Co-op was established in 1925.*

invariably dried about the end of May. In every locality there were the precious few that never dried – treasures almost on a par with gold mines. Farmers had to travel miles in those days to draw water for households and animals.

I remember we had what was known as 'the truck' – a low flat structure on wheels and capable of holding a 30 gallon barrel plus a smaller one. It was drawn by Jess, the donkey, a very strong willed female who, without difficulty could find her way to the well and back a mile away. Those of course were the days when the roads were traffic free and a motorcar was a rarity. The well, 'Tobar na bhFeochadain' was never known to dry in spite of the fact that there was a succession of customers from morning till night. The buckets of water had to be brought up six steps to the barrels. When full they were covered with clean sacks held down by a hoop and because Jess was a slow mover, little of it was lost in transit.

Going to the well was a way of life when piped water was an unknown quantity in country areas, before rural electrification brought a whole new dimension to the scene. When the breakthrough came (in the 1950's) many years and countless barrels of water later, it changed the whole aspect of rural living and made the hard physical work of man, woman and beast an unhappy memory.

Parents in the 1920's believed that busy children seldom got into mischief and without a doubt the well balanced lives we led, not having much in the way of luxuries or entertainment made us happy and contented and appreciative of the little extras as rewards, that came our way occasionally.

In the cold winter evenings cutting turnips for the cattle was a cold hard chore. The turnips had to be put in a machine and the handle turned to slice them, and transported into the stall and calves house in baths. But hardest of all the chores was 'bruising' furze for the horses. The furze machine was much like the turnip machine with a sharp knife like blade and a handle to turn. The finer furze was easy enough to handle – it was transferred from the heap with a wooden implement called a Gabhlog but when the blade hit a stump it was full stop and much effort to get going again. The horses, strangely enough loved it and Jess always got her ration. It was hard going to get all the chores done before dark – no ESB[37] then.

Fish and Fowl

The farmers in the 1920's had a great affinity with the land. They worked on it all day and at night around the fire they discussed every aspect of it. But there were a great many people in the area that had very little as regards property and poverty was rampant. One advantage the coastal areas had was the fishing and in those days it was big business; indeed it was the lifeline of a great many families in the parish. The fishermen shared six or eight oared boats and rowed out miles to the fishing grounds. They knew where the different species of fish were to be found – whiting, pollock, bream, mackerel and herring. In summer they often stayed out there three or four days or until the boats could hold no more. Their food consisted of yellow meal stirabout – the meal was boiled until thick and it cut like

---

[37] Electricity Supply Board

bread. That with water was the fishermen's diet. The fish was sold locally, or taken to Clonakilty. I remember my mother curing great quantities of it for winter. A great number of the people never tasted meat, but farmers usually cured their own bacon and what a treat it was when the pig was killed and the delectable fresh pork and pork steak was so enjoyed. There was always some for the neighbours and the remainder was salted and put in a barrel. My mother filled the puddings, after thoroughly washing them, with a mixture of oatmeal, onions, salt and pepper and blood and then boiled them in the big pot with hay in the bottom to prevent burning. They were so delicious and they were shared with the neighbours.

We seldom had lamb or beef; perhaps at Christmas, but when my mother went to town she always bought a big piece of boiling beef and with that she made dumplings and cooked them with the meat. It was food fit for a king and we did justice to it.

The farmers in those days were almost self-sufficient. Every farmer grew at least an acre of potatoes for their own use and for feed for pigs and fowl. They grew cabbage, turnips, onions and carrots, always enough for the year. Nobody would even think of buying vegetables. They had butter from the milk, and the wheat according to what was needed, was taken to the mill. There were lots of mills in every country area, some very old stone mills and they ground either coarse or fine according to taste.

Then there were the fowl. My mother kept about 100 hens, free range of course. Deep litter was unheard of then. As well as the hens she had turkeys and geese and ducks. She as was the custom hatched the eggs under 'clucking hens'. Usually a sitting was 13 or 14 eggs according to the size of the hen. Chickens took three weeks to incubate, turkeys and geese about four. The chickens were reared and fattened: the cocks (with the exception of the odd one for the table) were sold and the pullets kept replacing the old hens whose laying life was ended. The turkeys and geese were sold for the Christmas market and were a welcome source of revenue at a lean time of year. Turkeys were delicate birds and with the hazards of sickness as well as foxes you could truly not count them until you had the money in your hand.

Fun and Games

Our busy schedule left very little time for actual games in my young days. Those of us academically inclined and able to lay our hands on a book had great opportunities in the summer months when one of the regular tasks was minding the turkeys and chickens from the hawk and grey crow. We made daisy chains and fitted foxglove flowers (fairy thimbles) on our fingers. In the spring we looked for birds nests and vied with each other as to who had the biggest number. They were only to be looked at, not touched. We were warned that the mother bird would forsake the little ones if we did. The hedges and ditches were full of nests and alive with birdsong with no modern machinery or cars or trucks on the road to disturb them. The corncrake was 'on the air' morning noon and night and the young birds were often saved at hay cutting time and put in a safe ditch. See-saw was a favourite pastime. We put a heavy plank across a low ditch [38] and one sat on either end. We sang little songs like 'See-Saw, Jack in the Pool'. We had swings when we could prevail upon

---

[38] A stone or earthen wall, often vegetation covered.

an adult to tie a rope upon a strong branch. At school we played 'Ring a Rosie' and 'Spy' and 'Chickens come flock'. On wet days we danced in the classroom at lunchtime and at Halloween we had 'Snap Apple'. 'Shop' was always a favourite and our merchandise was limited to stones and bits of coloured glass and sand, which we used for tea and sugar. Those were the days when packaging and tins were unknown. We had sack races and played hoops and in our simplicity created a lot of pleasure and happy memories which will always be with us.

The Village shop

The shop cum Post Office, cum general store was almost a social centre for the area. It carried a huge selection of goods; grocery and provisions, bacon, dried fish, cups, saucers, jugs, basins, saucepans even knitting wool (Mahony's Blarney Fingering) for men's socks and long winter stockings for the young folk. One could buy ladies lisle stockings and little necessities like elastic and needles and thread. In the store attached there was coal and different kinds of animal feed like meal and bran and pollard. The only pretence of luxuries were the two penny packets of biscuits and quarter and half–pound packets of cream crackers and maybe the odd currant loaf.

Wednesdays and Fridays were hyperactive days at the shop. Wednesday was egg and butter day. The farmers brought the week's supply of butter and eggs and Paddy, the general factotum, packed the eggs between layers of straw into wooden crates and brought them in to the town to the egg store. He wrapped the slabs of butter in white cloths and they too were sold in the butter market. His form of transport was a pony and cart and he sat on top of the crates. Those were pre-creamery days and a barter system was in operation. The farmers and cottiers exchanged their produce for necessities like groceries, flour, animal feed etc. and very little money changed hands.

Business boomed on Friday, pension day. The pension at that time was ten shillings weekly, maximum, but in the twenties and thirties it provided the week's groceries for an average family.

The village shop did not provide 'special offers' in its services but it was friendly and personal, and when times were bad, which they invariably were, at that time credit was never refused. Each customer had a 'pass book' in which an account was kept in elementary book-keeping. At Christmas everybody got generous 'Christmas boxes' and often during the year there would be the odd currant loaf or pot of jam slipped into the basket. One wonders if we were better off in our simplicity compared with the present system.

We spent the infrequent pennies we could come by in a little sweet shop near the school. Two sisters (Coughlan) carried on a little business, really from a large press in their living room. Miss Coughlan made cones of newspapers and on a good day you might be lucky enough to get ten sweets for a penny. Sometimes they had caramels 'Colleen Kisses' and they were sheer heaven. There was no talk of calories in those far off days, just pure luxury unspoilt. Sometimes too they got drumsticks – a gorgeous chocolate covered hard sweet on a stick and at two for a penny they were the ultimate.

Travelling visitors

Every area produces its individual characters and West Cork was no exception to that rule. In my young days our unexciting lives were enlivened by the visit of one or other of the regulars who called once or twice a year and some of whom were given a bed on the settle for the night. One I remember always in my prayers was Sean O, a mild soft spoken man who worked with a farming family on the far side of Clonakilty. He had a brother in America who wrote to him every Christmas and sent him £5.00. My father wrote on Sean's behalf to thank him – it was an annual task. I did well on the transaction getting a whole shilling from Sean and indeed many a bag of sweets as well. He always stayed the night and was gone in the morning at sunrise – one of God's gentlemen, scrupulously clean, honest and God fearing.

A much more forcible visitor was Sean Sile. His travelling periods were interspersed with short holidays in a neighbour's farm where he paid for his keep by cutting wood, clearing overgrown ditches and tidying generally round the yard. Sean had a quick sharp tongue and when the Parish Priest lectured him about a 'rolling stone gathering no moss'. 'No father, he replied, 'but it has the scenery'. Jack (or Sean) was very partial to the locally brewed black drink with the creamy head and spent many a night in the 'guest room' of the Garda Barracks after a heated altercation with the officers of the law.

In complete contrast was the 'Soda Bread Man', a quiet unassuming Mayo man. He adored brown bread and only stayed long enough to take a few cups of tea and brown bread and butter with a piece of cake in his bag for the next day.

Kitty C was a lady with a touch of elegance. She always wore skirts almost to the ground and produced a bag from under her shawl, which contained needles, spools of strong black and white sewing thread and bits of coloured hair ribbon. It was to us children almost a Pandora's box and we loved to see her coming.

The 'foxy woman' was a tall well-built lady with a head of fiery red hair. She too carried a basket, with religious objects like small statues and pictures. She had, if my memory serves me rightly, sixteen children, and was always on the scrounge for a bit of tea and sugar, bread or anything wearable. She brought first hand news of relations of ours who lived at the other end of the country – her travels were extensive.

Then there was Johnny Polly. He was a survivor of the 1914-18 war and he told us of how he laid under a dead soldier and pretended to be dead when the enemy scouted around. Needless to say he always had a rapt audience and we got all the gory details of his precarious journey back to camp. His greeting invariably was 'Seldom I come' so we christened him this.

There were many other 'Knights of the road', each one highly individualistic. They had certain stopping off houses where they knew they were welcome and sure of a meal. They were colourful characters who brought a touch of adventure on their visits and always appreciated the hospitality they received.

St James Day

St James was the Patron Saint of Ardfield and his feast day was celebrated on the third Sunday in July. There was a holy well named after him in the area to which people went to pray and make rounds but I am afraid it wasn't the religious aspect of the feast that appealed to us children. Rather it was that traveling shops from Clonakilty came to the village on that day and great crowds gathered to celebrate. The goodies were displayed on flat carts covered with white sheets with an overhead cover to keep off the sun. For months before we saved every penny diligently and hoped it would be supplemented by the contributions of relations. A half crown[39] was the very most we could hope for and we had to budget carefully on the day to stretch it as far as possible. The sugar stick was the biggest draw. That came in the way of thick sticks of delight made from brown sugar and butter plus some secret ingredient known only to the woman who made it. It sold by the penny worth. There were packets of biscuits, big rosy apples, lemonade, a rare treat and partaken with big currant buns - bath buns as they were known. But the gooseberries were the greatest of all - big luscious mouthfuls of sheer delectableness. They were sold by the pint and the supply never lasted long. The young people danced on a cement platform to the music of a melodeon. There was often a game of football in the field across the road and a score of bowls which was always popular. The whole scene was so happy and relaxed and we looked forward to St James's Day for weeks before and even now, a lifetime after, we cherish the memories it invoked.

The Feast of Feasts

If anticipation is the greatest pleasure in life, the weeks leading up to Christmas were sheer heaven. December (Mi Na Nollag) the very name filled our young lives with

---

[39] Two shillings and sixpence (30 pennies) in one coin.

pleasure. The Christmas cards were bought and posted to America and the turkeys were brought in off the stubbles plump and ready for market. They represented the housewife's 'pin money' and their price determined the extent of the luxuries that could be afforded for the feasting. There was always great excitement when they were being taken to market by horse and cart in covered cribs, and many a Hail Mary went to them for a good price - at that time about sixpence per pound.

Christmas was the occasion of one of our rare visits to town. The shops were a glimpse of fairyland and the little money we had so diligently saved put us through agonies of indecision on how best to spend it. The shop keepers of that era gave their customers 'Christmas boxes' which included big fruity barm bracks, coloured candles and other goodies. It was a time of plenty but the old and needy were not forgotten and it was the pleasant task of us children to bring a little Christmas cheer into their drab lives.

The puddings would have been made earlier in the month and hung in their floured and greased cloths. Preparing and making them was a pleasant chore and we chopped and stirred and wished with gusto. The postman too was a welcome visitor, and because most people in the area had family in England and America, the registered letters were eagerly looked forward to and were a big help in the lean years of the 1920's.

Christmas cakes as we know them now were unknown except perhaps in the 'big houses', but we were lucky. A cousin of my mother's in Kildare sent us an iced cake every Christmas. That cake was the 'piece de resistance' of the festivities. We called it the 'Kildare Cake' and talk about it being precious! We each got a slice with lemonade on Christmas Eve while my father had a big glass of punch and wished us *go mbeirimid beo ar an t-am seo aris!* [40]

On Christmas Eve too we put up the decorations – the house had been scrubbed and cleaned on the preceding days. The paper chains and 'mottoes' with Santy's smiling face were put in place and the candles fixed in their decorated containers. We all went to confession and had fish and white sauce for dinner at dusk. At dusk too the candles were lit – to light the Blessed Mother and St Joseph on their journey. We loved going outside to see all the lights in the windows of own and the neighbours' houses.

We went to bed early, full of excitement, having hung our stockings on the chimney place and fearfully willing Santy, or Daddy Christmas, as he was then, to visit us. The light was not very bright as we crept downstairs to investigate the contents of the stockings. There was always something nice like a storybook and a coloured hanky, perhaps a little bag of sweets and an apple and orange. So little compared to today, but so much to our simple aspirations.

We went to Mass in the dark. Those were the days before electricity arrived and in the early morning the stars were as bright as they must have been on the first Christmas morning. Neighbours greeted one another Nollaig shona dhibh'[41]' and the music of the Adeste (Fidelis) filled the morning air.

---

[40] May we all be alive and well at this time next year.
[41] Happy Christmas to you all.

Friends and neighbours

A good relationship between neighbours is important in any community, but for farmers in those days it was an absolute necessity.

The system was that everything was shared – horses when needed for ploughing and harvest work, harrows, rollers, hay equipment. The smaller landowners couldn't afford much in the way of working gear but no field was left untilled or no crop unharvested for want of equipment.

But poverty was rampant and how families managed to survive with so little of the world's goods gets more mysterious the more I think back. It was quite usual to rear big families in one-roomed thatched cabins. I can recall one family who lived near us: father, mother and seven children. All father possessed was part ownership of a four oar boat and even though the fishing season was longer then owing to good summers, there was always the long winter and spring to provide for. It was customary too for farmers to give a few drills of potatoes to landless families in exchange for help at busy times, and there was always the jug of milk and bit of brown flour for the needy.

My favourite couple to visit were Dan and Mag. They were all right financially because they both had the pension, £1 weekly. I loved going down the road with the jug of milk and sometimes I got 2 pence, which was bliss and the reason, no doubt, for my eagerness to visit. Mag was unique, she kept hens and I declare to goodness she could reel off the pedigree of each of them almost like Herd Book cows nowadays. They had a cat called Cluasac and a little dog, Prince. Cluasac was partial to tender young chick and was in constant trouble. Mag had a dresser filled with magnificent china. When making tea she boiled it in a can at the side of the fire. It was so strong it could almost stand on its own, but if one was lucky enough to call on a Friday evening when Dan, and Kruger the donkey, brought the shopping, and Mag cut a big thick slice of fresh crusty bread and home made butter, that was something worth having.

On Sunday afternoons I usually went to a nearby house to play with the girls of the family. The mother, God love her, was crippled with arthritis and could only sit and 'blow' the fire machine with difficulty. She was an avid reader and had been in America before she married. A relation sent her books and she could tell the stories she had read better that any TV critic. I can remember sitting around the fire on cold Sunday afternoons and listening with rapt attention to tales of East Lynne and such like, while Mary, the eldest girl, who had to take her mother's place at an early age, baked a currant cake for the tea in the bastible. Happy days when our limited horizons did not inhibit us. We were content in our naivety.

The Attridge family lived in the 'Tower', a tall slate building on the highest point of the parish with a view of the coastline from Galley head to Kinsale. He was a Coastguard during the last years of British occupation and continued to live in the Tower after the Free State was founded. The 'lookout' on the outside of the building was the joy of our young lives and on our return journey from school we often climbed the twenty steps to the top. It was a worthwhile climb – the panoramic spread of sea and countryside was breath taking.

Mr Attridge pointed out interesting places and told us about the day the Lusitania[42] was sunk almost straight opposite the Tower. He was a keen gardener and often gave us some of his lovely ripe gooseberries and apples. He was also a great reader and his sons in England sent him the 'Daily Mail', which he always passed on to my father. We always looked up to him as the kind cultured gentleman he was

Memories, Memories

I can remember life even before the pony and trap when we went to mass in the horse and cart. There was a nice bed of straw laid in the bottom of the cart and a big sack filled with straw to sit on. Along with the fact that the cartwheels were iron shod and that the roads were only dirt tracks sheeted with small stones broken with a hammer by the County Council workers, it was anything but a smooth ride. It was a few years on before we got the trap with rubber tyred wheels and much more comfort.

Miss Galwey, who lived on one of the big houses rode in style in a covered car with the driver sitting on a high seat outside. Then came the first motor, owned by Colonel Longfield who lived in Dunowen House. That created some stir in the neighbourhood. Earlier on Lord Carbery of Castlefreke, on the far side of the parish terrified the citizens when he drove round the narrow roads. They called his car the 'headless coach' and jumped over the fences when they met him.

I saw the first bus when I was about nine years old. It came from Cork on an excursion to Dunnycove Regatta

---

[42] On May 7, 1915, the British passenger ship was sunk by a German U-boat.

and was the subject of so much interest that the regatta was ignored.

It was as all so very long ago in another life and another culture, but the winds of change were blowing across the Atlantic and a new way of life was gradually transforming the old pattern. The old neighbours were slowly passing away and many of the cabins were empty and falling apart. The district was poorer for their passing. They had all made their mark on the quality of country life.

1934

The second phase of my life meant the ending of National School, passing the Primary Exam, and going on to Secondary. Secondary School was known then as 'Secondary Top' and it meant cycling six miles each way to the Convent of Mary in Clonakilty town. The transition was traumatic. Living as we did so far from the town at the very end of the Parish, I had rarely seen a nun and the huge classrooms and equally big classes were overwhelming in the extreme. Bicycles in the 1930's were luxury items and needless to say I did not possess one, but getting to Clonakilty meant I had to have one. So with great excitement on my part and with much saving and scrimping on my parents I was the proud owner of a new bike. It was an Elswich complete with carrier, for my books and cost £15: a lot of money in the 1930's.

On my first day I was put through an extreme exam together with about 12 more country girls. The town girls who had been through Convent Primary were very slick and I'm sure laughed behind their hands at the country cawbogueses'[43]'.

---

[43] A disparaging term for country folk.

The number of books was huge as was the amount of work and I can still remember the first poem we had to learn off by heart in those days: the 'Burial of King Cormac'. Long and hard, as well as Irish poetry, Irish and European history, world geography, English grammar and literature and an extra language either French or Latin. Maths were the usual arithmetic, algebra and geometry. It was a formidable timetable, and a long day starting off from home at 8.15 am and getting back at 5 pm. The roads were rough, stony and littered with potholes. Twice a year they were sheeted with small stones and for weeks until they sank in a bit they were a nightmare to cycle over as well as disastrous for tyres. It was some years before steam rolling was introduced to say nothing of tarring.

As well as five full days we had half day on Saturday when we did drawing and Christian Doctrine. It took a few months and diligent application to get into the routine and a lot of midnight oil was burned to get through the homework.

In the 1930's the State exams were only beginning to be included in the school curriculum and Civil Service, teaching and nursing were about the only careers available for girls. One advantage of secondary school was that with the amount of homework I was not expected to contribute to the evening chores on the farm. While attending primary school there were a thousand jobs after school, in the autumn picking potatoes after the plough, helping my brother to slice mangolds and turnips for the cows, turning the wheel to cut furze for the horses and donkey, feeding the young calves after milking and carting into the house timber blocks which keep the fire going, getting the supper and washing up after in a dish of hot water from the kettle. How we have progressed since, with hot water at the turn of a tap, candles and oil lamps replaced with brilliant lighting and cookers and microwaves replacing the open fire and iron pots.

The summer holidays were eagerly looked forward to. It was so good to not to have to get up for school and any chores that had to be done were so much easier in the lovely long sunny days, where you would not need a coat from May to October.

Too soon September came and off on the road again back to school. The time passed and the knowledge grew, encouraged and helped by the good sisters dedicated to giving young people a future. I ended up in the Department of Trade and Industry in Dublin's Lord Edward St. I stayed in digs in Drumcondra and I cycled to work across the river. My wages were small and I had to survive on very little. Dublin then was a nice city where it was possible to walk unaccompanied at any time. For a few pence it was possible to go on the train to Bray or Howth or any of the interesting suburbs and when funds allowed, a cup of tea and a bun for 6 pence. In the winter there was such variety: the cinema, the Abbey and the Gaiety theatres. One could get to 'the Gods' (the very top seats, for a shilling [44] and 2 pence for a packet of sweets. Phoenix Park was a joy, the flowers and shrubs and lovely walks. Croke Park was one shilling and six pence for the side-line.

I remember September 3rd, 1939 when Cork and Kilkenny played the Hurling Final. That morning on the radio the British Prime Minister Chamberlain declared war on Germany. Life for everyone was much harder for the next six years. Most food stuffs were rationed: half an

---

[44] Twelve pence.

ounce of tea, 2 ounces of sugar only on ration books, no white flour or bread; clothes, candles, oil, all rationed but at least we were not involved in the awful war. Stories of the raid on Britain and of the thousands dead came through on the radio and somehow we kept out of it.

I left Dublin and got married back home in Ardfield: that was now the third phase of my life. I was back to farming, back to my roots. After the war everything took on a new aspect and in a few years things stated to take a new turn. For us country folk the electrification was a red letter day. The light meant that in winter every farmyard was lighted, milking machines were installed to ease the heavy chore of milking and every hand worked appliance was converted to electricity making life so much easier. Electric pumps brought water up from the depths in every farmyard and along with the 'power' tractors were appearing with attachments for all farm work. The days of the horse were fast disappearing, we were on the road to progress both indoors and out.

We had come through some hard times, times when money was scarce and we bartered farm produce for necessities. The country was settling down after years of internal trouble and our standard of living grew with the years, for better or worse, time will tell.

Lightning Strike[45]

The third of February 1963 started off like any other winter morning, dark and drizzly and bitterly cold. The cows were milked and Denny had gone to the creamery. Eileen had gone down to the yard to feed the pigs and attend to her horse. Suddenly, without warning, it got as

---

[45] Published in the Ardfield Rathbarry Journal No 4 2002-2003 p. 41

dark as night and the kitchen was illuminated by what seemed to be a hundred bulbs. At the same moment the thunder shook the house. That was it – one flash, one unearthly peal of thunder and devastation!

In total shock I tore out of the house, sure and certain that Eileen must be dead. Thankfully, I met her coming across the yard. She and the dog were in the tractor house when the [46]lightning struck, it made a hole in the ground just feet away from her. The horse had burst out the door and gone wild. When we went into the pigs' house, they were all dead and we didn't see the dogs for days after.

We got ourselves up to the house and it was then that the disaster was evident. Most of the gable wall was blown away. Inside the house the scene was horrendous; every plug and socket was blown out of the walls, the wires torn out of the TV and the phone in the hall was halfway up the stairs.

Our initial reaction was to sit down and burst into tears, but worse was still to come. We hadn't thought of the cows and it wasn't until Denny had come home from the creamery and went into the stall that the final blow struck. Two of the best cows, three year old Pedigree Friesians, were dead. Amazingly, another was still alive between them. They had been Denny's pride and joy, and he was grooming one of them for the Dublin Spring Show.

I can only compare the house to a wake-house for the next few days. All the neighbours and friends came to see the damage and to commiserate with us, still in shock. The help and service we got from the builder, the

---

[46] Eileen was about twenty years old at the time and says that she thinks the Wellington boots she was wearing saved her.

ESB and phone people was beyond words. Pat O'Sullivan came from Clonakilty with a team of men and material and they did a terrific job on the gable. The ESB worked all day and into the night and brought back power, and we had the phone a few days later.

But the psychological effect of the whole disaster was phenomenal. It took a long time to come to terms with what, was in hindsight, our Armageddon. Even today, fifty years on, I still feel physically sick when there is thunder or lightning, and I live again through that morning in 1963.

Rites of Passage

The following sections deal with common experiences of many local women in the twentieth century.

Birth

During the first half of the twentieth century babies were most commonly born at home with a doctor or midwife in attendance. The baby's abdomen was commonly bound with a strip of linen to protect the umbilicus and prevent herniation. Mothers were advised to spend ten days in bed afterwards, a practice that was abandoned later in the century when prolonged bed rest was known to increase complications like deep vein thrombosis. Mothers fed their own babies from the breast normally until the child was about a year old and sometimes supplemented that with a bread, milk and sugar mixture known as 'goody' until the baby was weaned gradually and began to eat normal food.

The baby clothes were hand made by knitting or hand sewing in most cases. Diapers were made from old sheets or flour bags and fastened with a safety pin. In those days many future mothers learned their childcare skills from caring for younger members of their own family.

Women had to be 'churched' before they could return to Mass. The following article explains the custom.
"Incredible as it may seem now, until the 1960s, many women who gave birth could only return to the church after they received a blessing from a priest. This 'churching' took place five or six weeks after the birth, purportedly so that the 'sin of

childbirth' could be washed away."[47] Thus the mother was not present at the christening.

In the 1960's the Second Vatican Council introduced a funeral rite for babies who died before baptism. This ended the heart breaking practice of them being buried outside the graveyard, in non-consecrated ground. Up until the 1970's it was also not uncommon for the Priest to veto the parents wishes for baby names and the names of saints or biblical references given preference.

Until late in the mid century It was an expectation of many men, and the church, that a woman's role was to produce a baby every year. This practice took its toll on the health of both mother and child although some found creative ways around this, for example by, 'housework or cooking late into the night until himself was asleep' or taking the train to Northern Ireland[48] for a supply of contraceptives[49].

Unmarried motherhood was considered socially unacceptable and girls were either sent to England if it could be afforded, or to the infamous Magdalene Laundries, where the girls were forced to earn their keep by working for up to two years after the birth. Their babies were adopted and often went overseas. Abortion is still illegal in Ireland.

Up until the 1960's it could be very hard for rural childless couples, because adoption might be vetoed by their own parents, if a farm was likely to be inherited.

---

[47] Irish Independent 13 December 2012 entitled, *Churching, labour and deliveries*
[48] Where the law of the Republic of Ireland did not apply to availability.
[49] Condoms or when available later, contraceptive pills.

In the second half of the century it gradually became more common for mothers to travel to nursing homes or hospital for the birth. In line with modern trends the lying in time was reduced dramatically, medical and surgical labour interventions became more common and breast-feeding unfortunately dwindled.

Marriage

While many people met and married for love, matches were still made for some rural couples up until the 1950's, especially if land was involved. Special 'matchmakers' would be employed to find a suitable spouse. The custom of a dowry being paid when a girl married, also persisted in some farming families. Part of the dowry paid would be used to assist in providing dowries for the bridegroom's sisters. There was a saying that, 'One dowry could marry a whole county'.

Most often church weddings were held in the morning and the couple would go away for a short holiday (if they could afford it) following a wedding breakfast with close friends and family in a local hotel or sometimes at home. Wedding clothes were most often those that could be used in the future for best because materials were often in short supply due to war and/or economic reality. The 'white weddings' of today were an innovation made fashionable by Queen Victoria and were not practical for most until later in the century.

Should the marriage not be a happy one, divorce was not an option until 1996. For many a rural woman marriage meant moving from her father's house to her husband's house, the only two homes she would ever know. However, rural Ireland had, and still has an unusually high number of people who, for lack of opportunity or the wish to, chose never to marry.

Death

Many of the traditions associated with death are still observed today. Although now it would be usual for the laying out to be carried out by an undertaker, rather than the local nurse or midwife, people both in town and country are still waked at home. The tradition of a person being laid out in a simple 'brown habit' persisted until around the 1950's but had fallen away in most instances later. The brown habit was thought to bring to the wearer special indulgences (such as less time spent in purgatory) if blessed by a priest with the dying person's hand resting in the habit.

In the traditional wake the clocks in the house were stopped at the hour of death and mirrors covered to protect against the effect of old superstitions that would bode ill for both the dead and the living. Special white embroidered or lace embellished bed linens would be used to dress the bed on which the body lay. Five candles, representing the five senses would be lit on a white draped table at the bedside, on which a crucifix and holy water would be placed. Neighbours and friends would come to the house to say the rosary and pay their respects and many would sit up with the family all night (and sometimes for several days) to ensure the person was definitely dead before they were buried. Considerable drinking of *poitin* [50] or whiskey and reminiscing would go on. Often in rural areas the funeral mass would be said by the Priest in the home and the body taken directly to the graveyard.

---

[50] Highly alcoholic distilled Irish beverage.

Undertakers and funeral directors took over many of the practical functions of coping with the dead in the Clonakilty area, after the mid twentieth century. Rooms were provided where those affected by the death could come to express their condolences to the family and say goodbye to the body in the open coffin. The rosary would be said and the removal of the body from the funeral home to the church the night before the funeral became common practice. Following the funeral, burial in the local graveyard is still the norm [51] and it is quite common for the distance from church to graveyard to be walked alongside the hearse. Special masses are held on dates one month and one year after the death.

---

[51] The old practice of burying unbaptized people, suicides, criminals and strangers at crossroads or in unconsecrated ground has been abandoned.

Legislation Affecting Women and Children in the Twentieth Century

Year	Legislation
1931	Legitimacy Act: allowed re-registration of children born prior to the marriage of their parents.
1937	Irish Constitution
1951	The Register of Adopted Children introduced
1957	Married Women's Status Act
1972	The Marriage Act: raised the minimum age for marriage to 16 years[52] (High Court approval needed to marry at a lower age).
1976	Family Home Protection Act
1979	Health (Family Planning) Act
1981	Criminal Law (Rape) Act
1987	Status of Children Act: allowed the father of a child to be named on birth registration where the parents were not married to each other.
1989	Judicial Separation and Family Law Reform Act
1990	Criminal Law (Rape Amendment) Act
1993	Criminal Law (Sexual Offences) Act
1994	Maternity Protection Act
1995	Family Law Act
1996	Domestic Violence Act
1995	Regulation of Information (Services outside the State for Termination of Pregnancies) Act
1996	Family Law (Divorce) Act
1998	Employment Equality Act

---

[52] From the age of 12 (bride) and 14 (groom).

The Role of the ICA in Improving the Lives of Irish Women

The Irish Countrywomen's Association (ICA) began in 1910 as a non-denominational and non-party political movement called the United Irishwomen (UI) founded by Mrs Harold Lett. Its aim was to 'to improve the standard of life in rural Ireland through Education and Co-operative effort'. Sir Horace Plunkett, the founder of the Irish Cooperative movement, influenced its ethos and saw women as the key to realising his movement's aims of better living for farm families.

Up to this point in time rural women had lives epitomized by exhausting work and privation. They had neither a vote, nor social life, nor anything to call their own. It was considered a radical idea to encourage women to go out of their homes and priests were reported as saying that, 'Women should stay at home and look after their husbands and children and not be going out to meetings'.

According to the ICA website[53], 'In the early days of the United Irishwomen, potatoes, cabbage and onions were about all the vegetables most people grew and ate. The UI bought a wider variety of seeds and encouraged women to grow a bigger variety of vegetables, and special vegetable cookery classes were organised. They also started gardens in schools. As the membership grew advice was also given on poultry and egg production, cow-testing, cheese making, and bee-keeping, and the initiatives resulted in better diet and nutrition and therefore improved health. One of the other results was

---

[53] www.ica.ie

the opportunity for women to generate their own income from selling the surplus products.'

The organisation changed its name to the ICA in 1935 and at around the same time, guilds were started up in towns as well.

In the 1950's electricity and safe running water were identified by the ICA as key amenities to achieve the Co-operative movement's aims of better living. The ICA initiated a campaign urging rural women not to marry a farmer unless he supplied running water in his house as well as his byre. As it says on the website: "He thought it a fine idea to put it into his byre, but 'why would you be bothered putting it into the kitchen – wasn't she well fit to carry a few buckets?' [was the] sort of attitude." An ICA poster of the time depicted two women carrying buckets. The slogan read, 'We did not promise to love, honour and carry water'. An ICA/ESB Model Farm electrical Kitchen was constructed in 1958 and then displayed around the country to demonstrate the ideal possible.

The ICA also made other huge contributions to women's health, welfare, and economic security, in part through adult education via summer schools organized from 1959 and later residential education through its own college An Grianan. They also encouraged rural tourism, Irish culture, arts and crafts, and established the Irish Country markets and the young peoples organization, Foroige, amongst many other accomplishments. The ICA is still active today in the greater Clonakilty area.

Women, tea and soda bread
Tea making and its consumption became a bigger part of the lives of the women in Ireland after World War 2 when tea leaves became more widely available and less

expensive. It was the drink of choice for women and a great thirst quencher for anyone expending a lot of energy working. The tea was (and is) nearly always served strong to ensure the flavour was not dampened by added milk. In the early days milk was added to keep the cost down and it became the widespread custom. Today the Republic of Ireland is the biggest consumer of black tea leaves in the world and the Irish *Barry's* or *Lyon's* tea always make most welcome gifts to members of the Irish diaspora.

Irish soda bread is as ubiquitous and delicious as tea. It consists simply of brown or white flour, salt, sour milk or buttermilk and soda. This can be assembled quickly (as it does not require kneading) and was baked as a round cake in a bastible over a fire before electricity, or as a cake or loaf in a tin in the oven since. Irish butter is liberally applied to each slice when cool.

This traditional bread rises exclusively with Bread Soda, other wise known as baking soda, or bicarbonate of soda. The question arises as to why this is so, and why yeast was not used as is customary in so many other places. The answer lies in the low protein composition of Irish grown wheat due to the cool damp climate.

A high gluten content is required for yeast to work. The characteristic light but chewy texture is formed when gluten in bread dough forms stretchy cells that expand to hold the gases produced by yeast. However, Irish wheat rises when lactic acid in the milk interacts with bicarbonate of soda to form tiny bubbles of carbon dioxide. It is thought that bicarbonate of soda was introduced to Ireland around the 1840's.

Miscellaneous Quotes

'A farmer's wife was preparing to feed an influx of hungry men working on the harvest. On going to collect the cooling bread she was horrified to see the cat had made a meal of it by eating the centres out of the brown cakes. What to do? Her neighbour suggested they slice and butter the remainder and serve it so. And so they did.'

'When electricity came to rural Ireland most of the crossroads ghosts disappeared.'

'There is a true story of a Co. Cork man who heard that his son was shot by the English in the War of Independence. He went to town to find his son. He recognised him from a distance (by an item of clothing he wore) amongst the dead being carried away. He had to go home and say nothing to anyone, because if it became known he was related to someone who had been shot by the English, the family home would have been burned down.'

An older neighbour was keeping turkeys. I asked her, 'Does it pay to keep turkeys?' She replied, 'Oh, never mind about that. It keeps the money together until Christmas'.

'I wanted to set up a First Aid group and asked a priest if he would come along and give it his support. His response, 'And who will be looking after your children while you are doing this?'

'A priest in the family is worth an outside farm.'

These stories only scratch the surface of what remains to be told. If you live in or near Clonakilty and would like to tell me your own story for a future volume please send me your contact details by email at:

abwickham@gmail.com

Clonakilty Post Office,
a former Presbyterian Church.